# THE LORDSHIP OF JESUS CHRIST

## WILLIAM H. PAPE

Published by Community Christian Ministries
Moscow, Idaho
ISBN: 1-882840-06-2

# Introduction

From June 1954 to July 1955 I was a junior officer on active duty on the staff of Commander Naval Forces, Far East in Yokosuka, Japan. I was also the local representative of the Officers' Christian Union. I inquired of several missionaries their recommendation for a Bible teacher for our Spring Bible Conference. Every person recommended Bill Pape. I remember riding with him on a train or bus in Tokyo and telling him that the subject of our conference would be the Lordship of Jesus Christ. He was not sure he could teach on this subject because all of his time recently had been in the Old Testament. He would wait on the Lord about it. The result was these seven messages from the book of Isaiah on the Lordship of Jesus Christ.

Mr. Pape was a missionary in S.W. China for seven years. During WWII Mr. Pape served as a chaplain for the U.S. Army Air Corp in Kunming, China. After a normal furlough return to China was not possible because of the change of government there. He then served as pastor of a Chinese Church in Tokyo. When that ministry was completed God led him to Germany to teach in the Brake Bible School where he has taught the last 20 years. He and his wife Dorothy continue to be active in The Evangelical Alliance Mission. They have each authored several books. His ministry has been much wider including a part time ministry as Far East Representative of the Officers Christian Union.

One of the extra motivations to reprint the Lordship of Jesus Christ is the celebration of the 50th anniversary of the Officers' Christian Fellowship of the U.S.A.

Jim Wilson
*Moscow, ID 1995*

# Preface for the Third Edition

In 1955 when serving as Pastor of a Chinese church in Tokyo, I was invited to represent the Officers' Christian Union (O.C.U.) as it was then called, in Japan.

At the second Far East Conference I gave seven messages on the Lordship of Jesus Christ, all taken from the Book of Isaiah. A chaplain at the Conference suggested that the messages would make a good book. This led to a writing career in addition to my basic ministry of Bible teacher. Moody Press accepted _The Lordship of Jesus Christ_ for publication. Other books, accepted by other Publishers followed - _I Talked with Noah_, _I talked with Paul_, _China Travail_, _She Called Him David_, _It Happened in China_ and _It Happened in Aruba and the Netherlands Antilles_. The last four were published by The Evangelical Alliance Mission of which I have been a member for 35 years. Copies of these are still available from the Mission headquarters P.O. Box 969, Wheaton, IL 60189-0969.

Moody Press decided against a second edition of _The Lordship of Jesus Christ_ but graciously gave me permission to republish the book. I decided to "go it alone" and a second edition appeared but lacked the promotion that a publisher gives. A Japanese translation was also made and published in Tokyo. The second edition eventually sold out, and now, to my own surprise, a third edition appears.

I repeat what I wrote in an introduction to the second edition. Since this little book first appeared "the world has become more turbulent, violent and explosive. In such unsettled times we need to be reminded that the power and authority of Jesus Christ our Lord has not diminished. Peace of heart and serenity of mind come from a firm conviction that Jesus Christ is in fact Lord of all."

**William H. Pape D.D.**

# Chapter One

*And in that day thou shalt say, I will give thanks unto thee, O Jehovah; for though thou wast angry with me, thine anger is turned away, and thou comfortest me. Behold, God is my salvation; I will trust, and will not be afraid: for Jehovah, even Jehovah, is my strength and song; and he is become my salvation. Therefore, with joy shall ye draw water out of the wells of salvation. And in that day shall ye say, Give thanks unto Jehovah, call upon his name, declare his doings among the peoples, make mention that his name is exalted. Sing unto Jehovah; for he hath done excellent things: let this be known in all the earth. Cry aloud and shout, thou inhabitant of Zion; for great in the midst of thee is the Holy One of Israel.*

*-Isaiah 12:1-6*

# CHRIST THE LORD AND SAVIOUR

ONE SINGLE ISSUE divides the world. The tides and currents of men's diverse opinions swirl around the maelstrom of whether Christ is Lord or not. Modern chaos and threatening conflicts are basically the outcome of this fundamental controversy concerning the position of Jesus Christ in relation to the human race. Men are not sharply divided as to the existence of a Creator. They are at variance as to one Saviour who is Christ the Lord. Except for an exceedingly small minority of uncertain atheists, mankind readily and unanimously accepts the idea of a Creator-God. Moslems have no quarrel with Christians on this point. Buddhists, for the most part, are also in agreement with us. Even the animist, bowing before rock and tree, dimly understands that there is One far above all that he worships. In the Western world rarely is a man found who does not believe in God. Even in the vast areas blighted by the pagan philosophy of Communism, the masses are allowed to continue their worship of God so long as religion does not conflict with duty to the State. Belief in the existence of God is not regarded as necessarily dangerous to the political system or threatening to the government. Ideas concerning Him are often grotesque, and worship is perverted, but some kind of recognition of the Creator is found universally. Indeed, it is on this basis that unity is sometimes sought. That we all worship the same God is advanced as a proof that all men are brothers.

Insist that Christ is Lord, and you divide the world. While God the Creator, in some way or other, is universally honored, Christ as Lord is not. In this sense He is not equal with the Father, and never will be until the day when He is given the name which is above every name, and every tongue shall confess that He is Lord to the glory of God the Father. Christ never has received the universal recognition that is given to God. His equality with the Father is the point that the world challenges and often denies. They will not give to Christ what they are prepared to give to God the Father. At Pentecost Peter demanded that Christ be recognized as Lord, and the true Church has been making the same demand ever since. But the truth has been bitterly resisted, and to this day Christ has not received the world's recognition as Lord.

For the Christian the matter has been settled, at least in theory. Christ is our Lord and Saviour. But

6

as to all the implications and full meaning of that simple fact many have only vague ideas. The need is urgent to listen again to this great truth emphasized by Isaiah so long ago.

Chapter 12 of his prophetic writing reveals, in words of classic simplicity, how Christ became our Lord and Saviour. Verse 1 states the need of salvation; verse 2 reveals how salvation was accomplished; and the last four verses of this short chapter describe the four results of salvation. In that order let us examine the matter.

"Thou wast angry" (v. 1). The anger of God is a fact. More than that, it is a fact that vitally concerns us. "Thou wast angry *with me*." God's anger is not a smoldering emotion within Himself. His anger is directed, and directed at us. The reason is not difficult to find. Although recognition of the existence of a Creator is universal, God is recognized only in a perfunctory way that differs very little from patronage. Few who admit there is a God are willing to admit Him into their lives. He is given credit for ruling the universe, but His right to rule man is denied. He is allowed to direct the stars in their courses, but not man in his way. His laws built into Nature are diligently sought and classified, but His moral laws are not so eagerly received. The only real conflict between science and religion is that science demands nothing of a man, and Christianity demands everything. Man, however, prefers to do as he pleases with himself, and everything else he can lay his hands on. Ruined cities, ruined bodies, ruined homes, and ruined society are a tragic comment on man's experiment in denying his Creator's effective control over him. As God surveys the wreckage, He is angry. Any other attitude would be toleration of sin. "To be angry and sin not" is just as possible as not to be angry and sin. If

7

God did not feel anger at the sin He sees in this world, He would not be righteous. Think of the injustice that some should wallow in luxury while countless others grow gaunt searching for husks. Think of the incarnate cruelty that drives lumbering tanks over the soft flesh of women and children whose only crime is that they love freedom. Think of the tyrannical savagery that has plunged the world into war. Think of the devilish psychological means used to rob men of their very minds. Consider the moral corruption in music, art, and literature that is defiling men in mind, body, and spirit. Look at the hell that man is making out of the paradise that God created. Consider all this and know that if God were not angry as He sees it, He would not be moral. In fact, His anger is toward those who have tampered with His handiwork, frustrated His plans, and ruined His creation.

One dull, wet afternoon in winter, long before the rain ceased, a roomful of toys of all descriptions had ceased to entertain the busy minds of two young children of a wealthy family. Since all legitimate games had been exhausted, only the unlawful remained. A bundle of comics, a pair of scissors, a jar of paste, and brand-new wallpaper provided the inspiration. Had the children known how much careful thought had been put into the choice of the paper by their parents, they might have been less ready to try and improve it. Had they known its cost, they would certainly have hesitated before adorning it with a variety of brightly colored figures cut out of the comics. And if they had thought at all of the probable reaction of their father, they would not have used the scissors and paste so recklessly that rainy afternoon. As it was, the experiment ran its full course. No parent in his senses would have applauded the shambles created in that beautiful room by two children in one short hour. The only possible reaction was anger. For anger is the opposite of pleasure. And angry their father was!

God's anger has four qualities which are often lacking in human anger. His anger is equaled by His grief. His anger is impartial. God's anger is also inescapable, and always compatible with all His other qualities.

In the days of Noah, as God surveyed the terrible consequences of breaking down the barriers between the holy and the unholy, and the danger that threatened the whole race because of the boastful violence and the persistent evil of human inventions in those times, His emotion as a mixture of anger and grief. "It repented Jehovah that he had made man on the earth, and it grieved him at his heart." In what sense did God repent? The word suggests a sigh. Early civilization was plunging downward so fast that it could be saved from self-destruction only by the swift obliteration of the evil forces within it. Since men would not separate themselves from their sin, they were committed to destruction with their sin. As God contemplated the great act of judgment that would destroy the world by flood, He sighed. Mixed with His anger at man's willfulness and persistence in sin was grief that judgment was necessary. How great that grief was can be measured by two other scriptures where the same word is used. When David received news that Absalom's ambitious rebellion had ended with the proud prince hanging lifeless from an oak tree, the brokenhearted king sobbed out his lamentation: "O my son Absalom, my son, my son Absalom! would God I had died for thee, O Absalom, my son, my son!" And the people said "The king *grieveth* for his son." There is an accurate picture of the heart of God as He sees the end of the wicked.

Anger at their rebellion is mixed with grief at their chosen end. Isaiah uses the same word (54:6) to describe the emotions of a young wife, rapturously looking forward to a happily married life only to find herself suddenly forsaken by her husband. God feels exactly the same about man whom He designed to be joined to Him for eternal mutual enjoyment. His anger at being faithlessly forsaken is equaled by His grief.

This particular quality of God's anger makes it righteous. Anger without grief may be impetuous bad temper: grief without anger may be folly. A parent who punishes a child in a sudden burst of uncontrolled anger is sinning. A parent whose heart is so tender that every disobedience is left unpunished, sins against God and against the child. If a child is to be punished without sin, the parent's anger at the wrong done must be equaled by his grief that the child misbehaved.

A missionary from China once had considerable difficulty with a servant who habitually pilfered the stores. There was often a tacit understanding among servants that "commission" not exceeding 10 per cent of the value of market purchases was legitimate, but this servant felt free to help himself much more liberally and a little too often. The climax came one day when he treated himself to a generous share of the missionary's fast-dwindling supplies. The long-suffering saint decided that the hour of reckoning had come, and her seething temper encouraged her to swift action. On the way to deal with the culprit, she happened to meet the pastor of the church to whom she poured out a torrent of complaints against her servant. What can I do with such a persistent thief?" she demanded, but the question was strictly rhetorical, for she had fully made up her mind as to what she was going to do. The Chinese pastor's unexpected reply however was full of divine wisdom. "Wait," he said, "until your sorrow that the man has sinned is equal to your indignation with his sin" Two hours of prayer in the quietness of an upper room were necessary before that balance was attained, but when at last anger and grief had been brought into a proper harmony, a servant was won for Christ, and the key of the supply cupboard was thrown away, never to be used again.

Second, God's anger is impartial, and directed against every kind of evil wherever found. God's anger does not vary from day to day or have regard to the status of the sinner. "He is angry with the wicked every day." That is His constant and unchanging attitude toward every selfwilled man and woman. Over everyone who does not obey the Son of God, the wrath of God hovers like an immense storm about to break and rain down destruction. The particular sins a person has committed are of little consequence, for there are no degrees of guilt. God is not so angry with the tyrant who murders millions that He has not time to consider the self-satisfied conceit of the Joneses—and all who try to keep up with them. His anger is not a mere capricious emotion, but the calm reaction of a righteous God whose displeasure has been willfully provoked. Sinners, who like to shelter beneath a cloak of religion, are no less immune from the wrath of God than the man who openly blasphemes the Lord. Status is of no account, for sinners have no status before God. The most eminent man loses his eminence in the presence of the Lord, and the most insignificant man loses his insignificance. God's anger is impartial to both.

The third characteristic of God's wrath is that it is inescapable. All through the writings of Isaiah is the terrifying refrain: "For all this his anger is not turned away, but his hand is stretched out still." It vividly de-

11

scribes the inescapable anger of God. The Book of the Revelation has an equally sobering passage. "And the kings of the earth, and the princes, and the chief captains, and the rich, and the strong, and every bondman and freeman, hid themselves in the caves and in the rocks of the mountains; and they say to the mountains and to the rocks, Fall on us, and hide us from the face of him that sitteth on the throne, and from the wrath of the Lamb: for the great day of their wrath is come; and who is able to stand?" (Rev. 6:15-17). Those words are not written to scare us. They are written that we might never know such a fear. God tells us the plain truth because He loves us and wants us to escape the judgment to come. Those who talk glibly of taking a chance should pause to consider such clear warnings. Since God Himself is inescapable, His anger likewise can in no way be avoided. A man might as well jump out of a plane at 50,000 feet, without a parachute, and talk of taking a chance, as speak of the possibility of escaping God's anger. No such chance exists. His hand stretches out until He reaches whomever He pleases.

God's anger is compatible with all His other qualities. Some varieties of modern apostasy illogically assume that God's love cancels His anger. Grief is supposed to drown wrath. It would be as reasonable to presume that humility negates courage.

A saintly old minister of the Episcopal church, well known for his outspoken evangelical sermons, was invited on one occasion to preach in a church where the Gospel was seldom heard. At the railroad station he was met by the curate who accompanied him back to the vicarage. On the way, the curate expressed the fervent hope that the visiting preacher would avoid such unpleasant subjects as Hell, judgment, and the wrath of God. "In that case," asked the pastor, "what subject do you suggest would be suitable for me to expound in your church?" "A message on the love of God, or something like that, would be most acceptable," replied the curate. The following morning, as the last stanza of the sermon hymn was being sung, the guest speaker made his way up into the pulpit and slowly turned the pages of the Bible. He announced his text as John 3:16 and began to read the familiar words with a dignified emphasis: "For God so loved the world, that he gave his only begotten Son, that whosoever believeth on him should not. . . " He paused, peered closely at the page as if bewildered, stopped abruptly, and then began to read the verse again. "For God so loved the world, that he gave his only begotten Son, that whosoever believeth on him should not..." A second time he stopped. Scratching his head in perplexity, he peered down at the curate to ask in a firm and clearly audible voice, "And now what shall I do, Curate?" The very verse that assures us of God's love, makes it equally clear that men who do not believe will perish. God's anger is as much a part of His eternal character as His love. He is angry because He loves, and He loves when He is angry. His anger cannot quench His love, and His love cannot annul His anger.

Emotions are stimulants to action. Fear impels men to avoid pain or danger. Love compels us to serve one another. Shame leads us to confession. True anger demands justice. Anyone who has watched bombs crashing down on defenseless cities of no military importance knows what it is to feel a deep anger that cries for justice to be done. Any man who could calmly read of the brutal slaughter of those Hungarians who counted liberty more precious than life, and not feel indignant anger rising within his breast, would be lacking in moral sense. Such anger is a vehement call for justice. In the same way, the wrath of God moves Him to deal with cruelty, injustice, oppression, inequality, lust, pride, and every other evil that violates His holy laws and brings untold suffering, sorrow, and sickness upon mankind. But if God were to deal with sin thoroughly, and His anger to fall on every guilty person impartially, who would escape? That is the practical problem we all face. "Thou wast angry with me." That constitutes the need for salvation which the past tense of the verb suggests has been provided. God was angry with us, but now His anger is turned away. The following verse explains how this miracle was achieved.

God's anger did not gradually cool down. It was not an emotional outburst that finally exhausted itself. His anger was born of His righteous nature that clamored for justice to be done. Therefore, God's wrath did not slowly subside. It swiftly fell. And fell on God Himself, for, "Behold, God is my salvation" (12:2). The dramatic style of Isaiah well suits this dramatic declaration. "Behold," he says, suggesting that we each look closely at this astonishing thing that has happened. God was angry with me: God is my salvation. He Himself has delivered me from His anger. And in this fact is the true reconciliation between the love and wrath of God. God is angry with every unbeliever. He is angry with you now if you are in that category. But His anger long ago fell on His own Son who, in the dark solitude of the cross, suffered the full and righteous judgment on your sin. He Himself became the Saviour.

Salvation is an old word, but not an old-fashioned word. It is old like such homey words as *mother, brother, man, moon,* and *plow.* In these days of general revolt, however, many of the old Bible words have been discarded for anemic substitutes. It was not that the old words were vague or ambiguous; on the contrary, they were too blunt and clear for modern tastes. A new vocabulary crept into preaching that spread confusion through large sections of the Church. This is well illustrated by an experience in the home of a lady who had the courageous idea of inviting all the ministers in town to a dinner at which she suggested a provocative theological subject for discussion She was herself a pastor's daughter which may explain her daring, or her sense of humor. As each of the brethren expressed his views on what should be required of an applicant for church membership, one of the guests innocently remarked, "In the old days, everyone had to be converted before he could join the church, but now, of course, it's different." The cause of this tragic mistake was easy to find. The pastor of the church to which the speaker belonged was "advanced" in his theology, and preferred a whole set of new terms to the blunt old Saxon words that had served the church well for at least four centuries. He would not speak of "being saved," but preferred to talk about "accepting Jesus' way of life." The change is significant. The new term delicately removes any suggestion that man is in a desperate condition of need, and instead offers for his gracious and noble patronage a way of life not very clearly defined. Many people quite naturally were delighted to learn that their pastors had discovered a new way into the church that avoided the humiliating necessity of confessing sin and being converted. The effect was just the same as if an old and famous university were to decide to scrap all entrance examinations and require that applicants have only a desire to enter the school. In the churches, such a policy created the utmost confusion. On the one hand were the old Bible words that even the most modern translations have not altered; and on the other hand were the new terms, liberally interlaced with psychological jargon, calculated to help people into the church without pain or discomfort. The theologian may claim that the new terms mean exactly the same as the old, but very few of the ordinary churchgoing people ever discover this. The remedy is not hard to find. It may be that old words such as *saved*, *lost*, and *repent* were misunderstood and misused by some, but the need is not for a complete set of new words that are so vague that scarcely anyone can understand them. The need is for clear teaching to remove misapprehensions and to establish the truth. After all, a great many words are grossly abused. The word *love* is an outstanding example. No man—theological expert or layman—even though he might have a violent dislike for such words as *saved* and *lost* would ever suggest that a substitute be found for it.

The word *salvation* is God's choice. It is found in thirty-two books of the Bible, and twenty-eight times in the writings of Isaiah. More than that, when God became intimate He chose for Himself the name Jesus which is the Greek form of Jeshua or Joshua. The name literally means Jehovah is salvation. We talk of "saving the situation," or "saving from defeat," or "saving money." God is concerned with saving men from sin and wrath. And to make that crystal clear He has made "salvation" part of His very name.

Verse 1 of our chapter (Isa. 12) declares that God's anger is against us. Verse 2 announces that God Himself saves us. In fact, God, and God alone, was the only One who could do anything about the situation. If God had done nothing, there was nothing that we could do. And if we could have done something, God most certainly would not have done the astonishing thing that He did. It would be neither moral nor righteous for one sinful man to offer himself as a substitute for another sinner. It would be neither righteous nor moral for God to forget about sin. In I Corinthians 5 Paul argues that the failure of the church to discipline a sinning member had made the whole church guilty. The little leaven of tolerated sin had affected the entire congregation. If God were tacitly to assent to sin by tolerantly doing nothing about it, then He Himself would become the chief of sinners. In fact, God did a unique thing that only He could do. He who is the Source of all justice, He who is both Law-giver and Judge, He who is the offended party, He it was who intervened by becoming a sinless man. He who decreed the sentence of death on sin, accepted our guilt and suffered the penalty Himself! "God is my salvation."

Isaiah is not merely stating a truth: he is also bearing testimony. "I will trust... He also is become my salvation" (12:2). By His death Christ justified His name and became the Saviour. That is an undeniable historical fact. That fact holds enormous potential for all mankind, but none automatically gains any actual benefit from it. His death was for all, but is effective only for those who believe. God became the Saviour by His own choice: He becomes our Saviour by our own choice. The Bible emphasizes again and again that faith which saves must be in Christ Himself. We are not saved by believing facts concerning Christ, nor by believing that the Gospel is true. We are not saved even by believing in the truth of the Scriptures. The Devil believes all that. We are saved by faith in Christ, our Lord and Saviour. The vital distinction between believing truths concerning Christ, and trusting Him personally is made clear in Ephesians 1: 1 3: "In whom ye also, having heard the word of the truth, the gospel of your salvation: in whom, having also believed, ye were sealed with the Holy Spirit." They heard the Gospel, and proceeded to believe in Christ. This truth must be stressed in these days when so many confuse an intellectual assent to the truth of the Gospel with a vital faith in the living Christ. In Oriental countries, such as China and Japan where much institutional missionary work has been done, there are thousands of people who have been "Christianized" by attending a Christian school where they learned, and readily assented to, many of the basic truths of the Gospel, but who have never trusted Christ as Saviour. Indeed, in those countries where pagan religions teach that faith comes through study, people popularly suppose that education in a Christian school and faith are synonymous. The Bible teaches differently. The faith that saves is an unconditional surrender to God. Man can set no conditions for his own salvation. For this reason, when by faith we receive Christ as Saviour, He also becomes our Lord. We have no choice in this for He is "our Lord and Saviour Jesus Christ" (II Peter 1: 11). If anyone intends to trust Him at all, then it must be on the basis that He becomes the Saviour from sin, and sovereign Lord. Many troubled men and women appear very willing for God to take over their problems, but will not agree to His taking over full control of their lives. They want a Saviour but not a Lord. Salvation is not on those terms. God is not a convenient, easy way out of troubles of our own making.

During the three years that the disciples walked with Christ, they usually called Him "Master" or "Rabbi." He was the teacher: they were the disciples. He was the leader: they were the followers. But after His death and resurrection, they entered into a new relationship with Him. This is evident from the new title they used for the first time. They called Him "Lord" (Mark 16: 19). By His death on the cross, He became their Saviour. By their willing acceptance of Him, He became their Lord.

The results of salvation are four in number: 1. the absence of fear (v. 2); 2. joy (v. 3); 3. thanksgiving (v. 4); and 4. testimony (vv. 5, 6).

If salvation in any way depended on our own efforts, we might well fear. The possibility would always exist that we had unconsciously offended God and so incurred His displeasure. Until the last moment of our lives the contingency would remain of a fatal mistake that could disqualify us from His favor. But since God is my salvation no such possibility of failure exists. No secret can be uncovered, for He knew all when His Son bore our sins. No successful accuser can arise from among men or devils, for God who justifies is greater than all. Nothing has been left uncompleted, for all God does is perfect. He who trusts Christ as his Saviour, therefore, ceases to fear. He does not fear that his sin will one day be uncovered, for it has been blotted out and forgotten by God. As far as God is concerned, it ceases to be a fact. He does not fear God's anger will one day burst upon him, for it has already fallen upon His Son. He does not fear sin's dark companion, death, for it has been conquered.

Fear and faith are mutually exclusive. He who believes does not fear, and he who fears does not believe. This provides a practical test of whether we have faith or not. A superficial observer might assume that in these days of scientific skepticism many people neither fear nor believe God. The alternatives of fear and faith cannot be avoided. If faith has departed from the earth, fear has come. And if fear of God has departed, a worse fear has come, for it is a hopeless fear that leads to destruction. A healthy fear of God is the foundation of sanity; an unhealthy fear of man is the road to insanity. It is this second type of fear that now spreads its gloomy shadows over the earth. Man is afraid of himself, afraid of his own inventions, and afraid of the course he has chosen. Statistics make this very clear. At the first meeting of Neurotics Anonymous, Inc., three years ago, the convention was told that there were at that time nine million cases of acute fear in the United States. "Men fainting for fear, and for expectation of the things which are coming on the world" is one of the great signs that will immediately precede the "Son of man coming in a cloud with power and great glory" (Luke 21:26, 27), and it is remarkable that our Lord Jesus, looking far into the future from His time on earth, mused "when the Son of man cometh, shall he find faith on the earth?" The earth filled with fear and void of faith are to be the last conditions of humanity. However modern man's fears may be analyzed and described, they all basically spring out of a fear of death with its consequences. Two factors make death terrible: the unknown future and the known past. The latter is worse than the former. No good reason exists for dreading the future except an uneasiness about the past. "The sting of death is sin." Accusing fingers from the past, haunting memories from yesterday, and prickings of the conscience all combine to take away any confidence that we might be able to stand before God unashamed. Such fears remain, like unwelcome clouds that cast a gloom over a bright summer day, until we trust in Christ implicitly and without reserve. Then we can "trust and not be afraid."

The second consequence of salvation is a natural result of the first. "Therefore with joy shall ye draw water out of the wells of salvation." Rarely does a person accept Christ without his heart being immediately flooded with such joy he never knew existed. Some years ago, one of the most regular members of a Bible class was a veteran of World War I. He had been a professional soldier who had seen much combat. How high he had risen in his career no one knew for certain, but we always called him sergeant, and the old man basked in the light of that unexpected glory. As his years declined, memories began to trouble him. His hands were stained with blood. In the service of his country he had killed in battle. That was no crime, but it worried him as he thought of giving an account of himself to God. Other things written into his record had less justification and increased his fears of coming judgment, and the courage of the battle-hardened old warrior began to fail. Together we slowly read the great promise of I John 1:7: "The blood of Jesus Christ his Son cleanseth us from all sin." The old soldier knelt, and in the plain, direct language of a fighting man confessed himself a sinner and asked Christ to save him. A moment later he was sobbing. Tears of joy fell as the fears and burden of a lifetime were suddenly removed. Like a thirsty desert traveler, coming suddenly upon a sparkling oasis spring, the sergeant with joy drew water out of the wells of salvation that day. His experience was not unique but the normal result of faith in Christ as Saviour. The third result of salvation is thanksgiving. "Give thanks unto Jehovah, call upon his name, declare his doings among the peoples, make mention that his name is exalted" (12:4). To realize what a glorious thing (v. 5) God has done to cause our thanksgiving, consider who He is, what man is, and what God has done.

In a later chapter we shall consider the greatness of the Lord. Here it is enough to recall that four unique adjectives needed to be invented to describe God. He is eternal, omnipresent, omnipotent, and omniscient. Those words are not just a bit of theology, but facts about God that vitally concern us. Put it this way. God knows all, for He has seen all from the beginning and to the end: He possesses irresistible power over all things and all beings, including you and me. But no words can better describe the greatness of God than the incomparable eloquence of the Holy Spirit speaking through Paul. Our Lord Jesus Christ is "the blessed and only Potentate, the King of kings, and Lord of lords; who only hath immortality, dwelling in light unapproachable; whom no man hath seen nor can see" (I Tim. 6:15). But even that magnificent sentence does not completely describe the full glory of the Lord. Human vocabulary is inadequate, as every man privileged to catch a fleeting glimpse of Him has soon discovered. After one swift glance at His terrible glory, they fell at His feet as dead, and said not a word.

A true description of man is almost as difficult as of God. Man himself is incapable of it. A camera might as well try to take a picture of itself. We accept the unbiased view of Scripture. "Man is without hope. His mouth is full of cursing and bitterness. There is no fear of God before his eyes. There is none that seeketh after God; they have all turned aside, they are together become unprofitable, there is none that doeth good, no, not so much as one." Evidence abounds on every side in support of that description of man. We find ourselves without excuse. Even the rationalizations with which we commonly comfort ourselves do not seem worth uttering in the presence of God.

As boys, my brother and I shared a bedroom. We enjoyed each other's company but not to the point where we could not enjoy a friendly fight. Many a night, long after we were supposed to be asleep, we battled it out with pillows as weapons. A pillow can do little damage unless it comes in contact with a hanging electric light. That is what happened. The room was sud-

22

denly plunged into darkness as glass rained down upon us. We slid back into our beds, covered with wreckage, waiting with pounding hearts the arrival of our father. Bounding footsteps heralded his arrival. He switched on another light and looked at us. The cord from the broken light was still swinging gaily in midair. More glass lay about the room and over us than anyone even imagined could have been contained in one electric bulb and its shade. It was useless to persist in pretending to be asleep. We looked up at our father. Even if we could have blamed an earthquake for the wreckage, we could not have been expected to sleep through it. An awful helplessness crept into our hearts. There was absolutely nothing we could say, not one single word of excuse. Even the inventive minds of young boys failed to produce a plausible reason for the ruin. We were as silent as we were guilty. And so are you and I before the eternal God who knows all and is everywhere.

Think of what God has done that is so marvelous. Let us imagine that a world conference was called to try to find a solution for the problem of sin, and let us imagine that one delegate proposed a plan which he was sure would save mankind. The plan was generally approved, and in some miraculous way, the delegate was sent to Heaven to present the plan to God. There he stands, this delegate, and begins to speak. "Our plan is simple but unusual," he says. "We would like to ask You to leave Heaven and come down to our world. As to the manner of Your arrival, we suggest that You be born in exactly the same manner as we are, except that Your mother will be a virgin. You will pass through a normal boyhood, and finally become a mature Man. We then suggest that You take our sins and regard them as if they were Your own, and so die instead of us. As to the manner of Your death, we have decided that it should be upon the kind of cross the Romans commonly use for the crucifying of criminals. After death, You will be buried for three days, and then You may arise from the grave and come back to Heaven after remaining on the earth for 40 days. In this way we are sure that an effective remedy for sin can be found." If such had ever happened, surely all the angels would have stopped their ears that they might not hear such audacious blasphemy. That God should become man! That God should have contact with evil! That God should die! In fact, such ideas never entered the mind of man. God thought of it. God, who is all that He is, died for man who is all that he is. Was anything more excellent than this? "Sing unto Jehovah; for he hath done excellent things" (12:5). Whenever the full light of this amazing truth pierces a man's understanding, thanksgiving will surge through his heart like the flood tide.

The fourth result of salvation is testimony. "Let this be known in all the earth. Cry aloud and shout, thou inhabitant of Zion; for great in the midst of thee is the Holy One of Israel" (12:5, 6).

The truths in this chapter of Isaiah are so well known that it seems almost unnecessary to write about them. They are part of every believer's basic knowledge. But everyone is not familiar with them. And certainly not everyone who is familiar with them shouts out the good news. Without any qualifications, we can say that the death of Christ upon the cross for us sinners was the most tremendous event in the history of the world. Pile adjective upon adjective, add emphasis to emphasis, multiply words by words, and use all the accumulated knowledge and eloquence of every orator of all ages, and you will not have an adequate vocabulary to tell what God accomplished through Christ on that dark day at Calvary. News heard over the radio is insignificant in comparison. No newspaper has ever carried headlines so astonishing. It would seem an impossibility to keep such news bottled up, and yet Isaiah found it necessary to encourage people to make it known. The Gospel was never intended to be a cherished secret known only to a few initiates. God's purpose is for it to be broadcast with a billion kilowatt power. This is not to be understood as a command to stand at every busy intersection and bellow out the Gospel message, but certainly the Lord lays on each of us a clear obligation to make the good news known to our friends and neighbors. It never entered the minds of the first Christians to keep their faith a secret. They shouted it out.

Christ Jesus, then, is our Lord as well as our Saviour by virtue of the salvation He accomplished by His death. When by faith we receive Him, fear is replaced by joy, and by the compulsion of a thankful heart, we pass on the word to others.

Before we turn our thoughts to another chapter of the prophecy, let us pause a quiet moment to make sure that He is our Saviour and Lord. Notice the change of tense in verse 1. "Thou wast angry with me, thine anger is turned away." God's anger turns away when we turn to Christ and ask Him to become our Saviour indeed. If you have never yet definitely turned to Him, now is your moment of choice.

# Chapter Two

*In the year that king Uzziah died I saw the Lord sitting upon a throne, high and lifted up; and his train filled the temple. Above him stood the seraphim: each one had six wings; with twain he covered his face, and with twain he covered his feet, and with twain he did fly. And one cried unto another, and said, Holy, holy, holy, is Jehovah of hosts: the whole earth is full of his glory. And the foundations of the thresholds shook at the voice of him that cried, and the house was filled with smoke. Then said I, Woe is me! for I am undone; because I am a man of unclean lips, and I dwell in the midst of a people of unclean lips: for mine eyes have seen the King, Jehovah of hosts.*

*Then flew one of the seraphim unto me, having a live coal in his hand, which he had taken with the tongs from off the altar: and he touched my mouth with it, and said, Lo, this hath touched thy lips; and thine iniquity is taken away, and thy sin forgiven. And I heard the voice of the Lord, saying, Whom shall I send, and who will go for us? Then I said, Here am I: send me.*

*—Isaiah 6:1-8*

# CHRIST THE LORD OF THE ANGELS

IN THIS GREAT CHAPTER Isaiah uses a name for God which is now seldom heard, and not always understood. He is Jehovah Sabaoth, the Lord of Hosts. The name was first used in the time of Samuel, whose father Elkanah annually went up to Shiloh to "sacrifice unto the Lord of hosts" (I Sam. 1: 3). In one place (40:26)

26

Isaiah refers to the stars as the host, but usually he uses the word to describe the company of angels. The term, in fact, means a mass of persons organized for war. That explains the significance of Jacob exclaiming, "This is God's host" when he was met by the angels of God at the time of Esau's approach with his armed host.

Here we are particularly concerned with the attitude and testimony of the angels. Isaiah's experience on that memorable occasion of seeing the seraphim is described in three succinct phrases. "I saw" (v. 1); "I said" (v. 5); and "I heard" (v. 8). These three declarations must be set against three facts concerning holiness as revealed by the angels. These are holiness declared (vv. 1-4); holiness needed (v. 5); and holiness bestowed (vv. 6-9).

The year of Uzziah's death coincided with the birth of Romulus, founder of Rome. His death was a tragedy that eclipsed the brilliant beginning of his reign. From the day that he exceeded his royal privileges and tried to usurp the priests' prerogative of offering up incense in the house of God, he declined to the dishonor of a leper's death. In the year that that king died, Isaiah saw another King. Few have seen the Lord as Isaiah saw Him. God has withdrawn a little from the human scene. He is here, but no longer openly as He once was in the bright days before sin entered the world. Since that time God has made Himself visible only to a small, select company: Moses, Ezekiel, Elijah, Daniel, and Isaiah in Old Testament days, and Stephen, Paul, and John in the New Testament economy.

The throne on which God sat was in the temple. An elaborate ritual was necessary before a few, highly privileged, Jewish priests could enter the earthly temple. Indeed, the inner part in which glowed the mysterious Shekinah glory of the Lord was seen only once annually by one man. King Uzziah, who had tried to crash his way in, had found the holiness of the place so devastating that he had emerged a leper. No man, except at peril of his life, dared intrude upon that sacred spot. For God, however, the temple is His ordinary dwelling place. He needs no preparation to enter, but by dwelling there makes it holy. This, of course, refers to the heavenly temple much more than the earthly counterpart. The throne in the temple was not upon earth, but "high and lifted up." God and His throne were separate from common things. He appeared as in another world. Some oriental languages have words meaning "elevated" or "lifted up" which are used when a gift is given. The basic idea is that the gift, by being given to a person who is politely regarded as far superior to the donor, ceases to be a common object. Its character changes. It becomes special. It achieves a uniqueness by being elevated to the category of a gift. In a similar way God is high and lifted up. He is altogether of a different order from all others and from all else.

Thousands of travelers are daily discovering the beauty of a world above the clouds. As the plane climbs swiftly, much of the unpleasantness of this earth disappears. The plane "high and lifted up" is in another world of pure and fleecy whiteness, arched with a limitless blue, and where the confusion, dirt, and noise, and all the gaudy ostentation of what passes for civilization cannot be seen nor heard. In that bright, cloudless atmosphere there is a strange sense of coolness, purity, and eternity. This dimly illustrates how God is high and lifted up. He is different from all others, in a position that is uniquely and exclusively His. "His train filled the temple," so that He, and what was His, alone filled that supremely holy place.

God's uniqueness must be remembered if holiness is to be understood. The attitude and testimony of the angels confirm this. Isaiah saw the seraphim. Even in the army of the Lord of hosts there is rank. Archangels, seraphim, cherubim, and angels—all are mentioned in Scripture. Little can be known about the seraphim because little is revealed. The word occurs only three times in Scripture: here in our chapter and in two other places where it is translated very differently. The first time we read of seraphim is in the story of the serpents sent into the camp of the grumbling Israelites. As a remedy for the deadly bites, Moses was told by God to make a "fiery serpent'" of brass and set it on a pole (Num. 21:8). The word literally is *seraphim*. The same word is translated in exactly the same way in a later chapter of Isaiah. In a prophecy against Philistia, Isaiah declared: "Rejoice not, O Philistia, all of thee, because the rod that smote thee is broken; for out of the serpent's root shall come forth an adder, and his fruit shall be a fiery flying serpent [seraphim]" (Isa. 14:29). The root meaning of the word is "burning," with its suggestiveness of brightness. If we cautiously push a little beyond what is revealed to try and find a connection between *seraphim* and *fiery serpents*, our thoughts lead us to Satan who once was one of the greatest of the heavenly creatures, and who, in his first dealings with man, took the form of a serpent. At that time, before the curse stripped it of its glory, the serpent was undoubtedly a magnificent creature, perhaps possessing wings and possibly the most beautiful of the animal kingdom. The high honor in which the winged dragon is held in Chinese and other ancient mythologies is suggestive that once the serpent, in a form different from its present repulsive appearance, was the greatest of the animals. Here, then, may be a clue that Satan himself was once a seraph, standing in the very presence of God, and created, like the seraphim, for the spiritual blessing of mankind. Certainly, even after his expulsion from the heavenly courts, he was able to appear there, no longer as a ministering spirit, but as an accuser of the saints, including Joshua, the high priest, and Job. If this be true, then we have an explanation of how seraphim could be used as a term for the highest of the angels, and for the highest of the beasts. Satan has been both.

We are not however primarily concerned with the office and nature of the seraphim, but with their attitude in God's presence, and their words of testimony. From these we learn some basic facts concerning holiness.

The seraphim were "above him" (6:2). They hovered above God, their wings fluttering in eager anticipation of His smallest commands. If He is the Lord of hosts, then those He commands are committed to instant obedience. Holiness calls for nothing less. Calling Christ Lord cannot be obsequious flattery. He carries no empty title.

In a small town away off in a remote mountainous part of western China lived a professional beggar who managed to wear his rags with an easy elegance that casually suggested he had once moved in much higher society. Perhaps he had. In keeping with his stylish tatters, he had a persuasive eloquence that always began with a string of complimentary titles calculated to stimulate a warm feeling of generous pride in the coldest heart. He attributed to people not much better off than himself honors that encouraged them to think of themselves as persons of rank, power and, above all, charity. But you cannot talk to God like that. In words of gentle, yet pointed, rebuke, Christ turned to His disciples with the very pertinent question, "Why call ye me, Lord, Lord, and do not the things which I say?" (Luke 6:46). Holiness is not correct Christian phraseology, but an unreserved commitment to unquestioning obedience to whatever the Lord requires. It is waiting quietly before the Lord to learn what He wants. The seraphim fluttered above the throne of God from whence His commands went forth.

"Each one had six wings; with twain he covered his face, and with twain he covered his feet, and with twain he did fly." These glorious beings used their wings to hide themselves as well as to fly. They neither asserted nor displayed themselves, but from behind the soft shelter of covering wings they proclaimed that God is holy. The attitude of these nameless seraphim, speaking always and only of God, exactly illustrates the true nature of holiness. Whoever speaks of himself knows nothing of holiness. He who claims that he has attained to heights unreached by others, or seen what is veiled to the unprivileged, has yet to learn what true holiness is. Holiness means self-effacement. Holiness will aim to hide self by all means, and to draw attention to the Lord. The man of the world speaks of the world. The spiritually proud Pharisee, ancient or modern, speaks of himself. "I thank thee that I am not as other men." The holy man speaks of God.

The song of the seraphim reveals another fact that cannot be stressed too much, for they themselves gave it a triple emphasis. "Holy, holy, holy, is Jehovah of hosts." Let us put this basic truth in the simplest possible form. God is holy. That is, He is not merely a little better than we, for He is "high and lifted up." Between Him and us there is an infinite and immeasurable difference in character. He, and He alone, is exclusively holy. "Thou only art holy" (Rev. 15:4). Holiness, therefore, must come from God. It is not an improvement

31

on anything human: it is essentially divine. It is not, and cannot be, the work of man or a human achievement. "Holy men" of heathen religions, who gain their reputation by lying on beds of spikes or walking through fire, are not much farther from an understanding of the truth than those who imagine that holiness is no more than the sloughing off of a few evil habits and the accumulation of one or two new qualities until the comparatively small gap is closed between what they are and what God is. No man made himself holy.

"And the whole earth is full of his glory." Glory is manifested holiness: holiness is glory veiled. In one brief phrase the seraphim made known that God's unchanging purpose for this world is for it to be filled with His glory. The heavens even now constantly declare His glory, but this earth, and man in particular, has failed to be what God intended. Any true understanding of holiness must start at this point. We are to be "filled with his glory." That is, holiness is a divine operation by which God's glory shines out through earthly, human vessels. How exactly does this take place? When we believe in Christ as our own Saviour, God cleanses us from all sin, and into our clean hearts He sends His holy Spirit. His Spirit is no mere vague influence, but God Himself who changes us "from glory to glory" (II Cor. 3:18). God does in us what we could never do: He makes us holy. This is not one sudden and miraculously complete transformation, but, as the Scripture clearly indicates, a gradual process by which we go "from glory to glory." The words of the Apostles' Creed can help us here. "I believe in God the Father Almighty, maker of Heaven and earth"— that is the beginning of spiritual understanding. "And in Jesus Christ His only Son our Lord"—that is the beginning of the Christian life. "I believe in the Holy

Ghost"—that is the beginning of a holy life.

> May His beauty rest upon me,
> As I seek the lost to win,
> And may they forget the channel,
> Seeing only Him.

These then are the qualities of holiness revealed to Isaiah as He saw the Lord of hosts. Holiness means being committed to unquestioning obedience, and not merely calling Christ Lord: holiness draws attention to God, and never to ourselves and holiness is a work of God by His Spirit, and never a human achievement.

Second, this chapter presents the need of holiness. When Isaiah saw what he saw, and heard what he heard, he cried out in broken words of confession: "Woe is me for I am undone: because I am a man of unclean lips ... for mine eyes have seen the King, Jehovah of hosts." It would be a mistake to think that Isaiah's ministry before this great experience was a complete failure. The first five chapters of the book were all spoken in the power of the Holy Spirit, and in them are to be found some of the most magnificent passages in the whole of the Bible. The first chapter contains the gracious invitation: "Come now, and let us reason together, saith Jehovah: though your sins be as scarlet, they shall be as white as snow; though they be red like crimson, they shall be as wool." Chapter 2 contains the promise of that glorious day when "they shall beat their swords into plowshares, and their spears into pruning-hooks; nation shall not lift up sword against nation, neither shall they learn war any more." (All the military colleges will go out of business when those days dawn) The third chapter has the assuring promise for the righteous that "it shall be well with him," and the fourth chapter prophesies of the coming of the Branch of Jeho-

33

vah who shall be beautiful and glorious. And chapter 5 begins with the exquisitely tender song of God's love for His people. God gave the word, and Isaiah spoke it faithfully. However, it is true that whereas in chapter 5 he calls out, "Woe is them," in chapter 6 he exclaims, "Woe is me." A new experience of the Lord made an indelible impression upon him so that neither he nor his message was the same again. So strongly was God's holiness impressed upon the prophet that he, almost alone of the Old Testament writers, refers to the Lord as "the holy One of Israel." Only twice in the writings of Jeremiah and three times in the Psalms is this name found, but Isaiah uses it repeatedly. Significantly, this descriptive title is mentioned twelve times in the first thirty-nine chapters of the prophecy, and seventeen times in the last twenty-seven chapters, which is part of the conclusive evidence that Isaiah was author of the whole book.

God's holiness affects us in a practical way more than any other fact concerning Him. His holy nature is the moral core of the whole universe; and the ultimate standard by which all creation will be measured. If God were not holy, we would not be sinners. The reverse is also true. God's eternal nature and His omniscience, for example, do not bring a wholesale condemnation down on our heads as does the fact that He is absolutely holy. Forget or ignore this truth and man appears in a much more favorable light in which he finds it easy to justify himself and all his works. This is exactly what has happened. Because men have forgotten or refused to believe that God is holy, the world has deluded itself into thinking that it is less sinful than it actually is. But if our ideas of God have changed, He has not, and sooner or later everyone is made to realize that the Lord is holy, either in the gentle light of scriptural revelation or in the shining glory of His awful presence.

"Woe is me for I am undone." What did Isaiah mean? In those days when fear of God was greater than now, men were convinced that to see Him meant death. As Isaiah became aware of the awful nearness of a holy God, panic gripped his heart and he cried out in dismay, believing himself lost. The experience was not an exhilarating ecstasy, but a shattering moment of misty confusion. "The foundations of the thresholds shook at the voice of him that cried, and the house was filled with smoke." Isaiah became acutely aware of his lips. He was a prophet; that is, one whose mouth utters the words of God. His lips, therefore, were the chief means by which he fulfilled his call and ministry. The divine name had been much upon his lips, but when he heard the seraphim speak, and clearly saw the Lord, he realized how deeply unworthy he was even to mention that holy One. When Isaiah saw God as He is, he saw himself as he was. His lips had become like those of the people to whom he ministered. "I am a man of unclean lips, and I dwell in the midst of a people of unclean lips" (v. 5). The lips of the seraphim were holy like those of God; the lips of Isaiah were unclean like those of the people. Uncleanness is here in direct contrast to holiness. What is not holy is unclean. The holy is that which is "high and lifted up"; the unclean is like that in the midst of which we dwell.

Let us thoughtfully apply this to ourselves. Among Christians, especially those active in the church, the name of the Lord is often upon our lips. "The Lord led me"; "The Lord told me"; "The Lord blessed me"; "The Lord wants me"; "Praise the Lord"— these and similar phrases are constantly heard when Christians meet for fellowship. But does the holy name always pass over holy lips? It is tragically easy for our mouths to become soiled. Isaiah surely had not fallen into the habit of using filthy language, but there was no clear distinction between the way he talked and the common speech of the people. It was not holy conversation: it was common parlance. Few habits are easier to copy than patterns of speech. Cliches are easily born, and multiply rapidly. A careless Christian can unconsciously pick up the world's current phrases, and repeat them without any thought that he is thus soiling lips that are meant for God's use.

Off the east coast of Japan a powerful stream surges steadily northward. A passenger on a ship approaching port can see no evidence of the current flowing across his route, but if the ship's navigator carelessly failed to take the stream into account, he could find himself many miles off course in a matter of hours. Worldly speech is as insidious as that current. Those of us who have spent much time among the fatalistic people of the Orient know how easy it becomes to assent readily to the common conception that nothing can be done about a situation. The Hindu or Buddhist, steeped in a hopeless philosophy, throws up his hands in despair and exclaims a thousand times a day no solution can be found to his particular problem. If we are not careful, we agree with him, forgetting that God can always do something about any situation. In the Western countries, we almost as easily pick up and use the popular cliches. Some are harmless and amusing. Others are part of a flood of senseless and untrue propaganda that defiles the lips of each one who passes them on. Paul warned the Ephesian church against "filthiness, foolish talking, and jesting." Foolish talking, in that verse, could be translated "moron talk." It well describes much that passes for conversation in these modern times. In some circles the level of conversation has fallen so low that men and women can think of nothing at all to say without first stimulating their turgid brains with alcohol which, in turn, enables them to mouth out gay nonsense unworthy of a child of six! Jesus bluntly warned that "every idle word that men shall speak, they shall give account thereof in the day of judgment" (Matt. 12:36).

Sin often has a focal point. For Isaiah, it was his lips. For us it may be the same. Or our cry may be different. Sometimes it is the mind that is unclean, or the heart, or eye, or motive. Even for a minister of God, of the eminence of Isaiah, the possibility exists of becoming defiled in these ways. We live in a sordid, dirty world. If only the absolutely pure in heart, thought, and deed were allowed to utter the name of the Lord, many of us would be silent, or else would cry out with Isaiah, "Woe is me!" Such a confession is never easy to make. At the time the words burst out from Isaiah's mouth, he was probably conscious only of the presence of God and the seraphim, but if any of his congregation heard the confession they were surely astonished. If reputation and prestige are considered, none will ever cry "Woe is me"; but if holiness is sought, the need for it must be confessed.

Now consider how cleansing was made, and holiness bestowed (6:6-9). If Isaiah were acutely aware of his need, God realized it even more clearly. Indeed, the Lord saw the need before Isaiah himself was conscious of it, and granted him the vision to make him realize his need.

The words of confession had hardly come to an end when one of the seraphim acted. He took a coal from off the altar. The great altar on which the sin-offering was made was in the courtyard outside the earthly temple. The altar of incense was inside the temple, and therefore it must have been from there that smoke ascended to fill the place, and from it that the seraph took the burning coal. The significance is that Isaiah was not in need of an initial, general cleansing from sin, but rather of a local application. "He that is bathed needeth not save to wash his feet, but is clean every whit" (John 13:10). The sacrifice of our Lord Jesus upon the cross was perfect and complete. His blood does cleanse from all sin, and any man, without any exception whatsoever, who comes to Christ, in any condition whatsoever, can be made righteous through faith alone and so fitted for the holy presence of God. But only a very presumptuous Christian would pretend that he could walk through this evil world without the slightest trace of defilement. Subsequent sins never endanger our salvation, for it depends on Christ's finished work, and not upon the efforts of man. But subsequent sins can spoil our testimony, extinguish our joy, destroy our peace, and, what is worst of all, make us unfit for the service of God. But provision has been made for this very emergency. It was tragic that the great Isaiah ever had to cry, "I am a man of unclean lips"; but the tragedy would have been greater if he had remained in that condition. Two dangers face every believer. One is to take advantage of grace and continue in sin; the other is not to take advantage of grace, and continue unforgiven. The first danger is real enough for Paul to take time to deal with it thoroughly in Romans 6. The second danger is no less real. Many a child of God has struggled long with a troubled conscience, or worried continuously over a sin that the Lord was ready to forgive and cleanse as soon as confession was made. If Christ commanded Peter to forgive his persistently erring brother seventy times seven, then He Himself must be no less ready to forgive as often.

38

The seraph flew to Isaiah. The need was urgent: cleansing was made with speed. God did not abandon His servant to hours of fruitless remorse. The live coal was ready on the altar, a seraph was waiting the word of command from the Lord of hosts, and cleansing swiftly followed on confession. "Thine iniquity is taken away, and thy sin forgiven" (v. 7). That was the process preparatory for holiness.

As soon as Isaiah's lips were cleansed, his ears were opened. "I heard the voice of the Lord" (v. 8). He overheard a divine soliloquy. The words heard were not spoken directly to Isaiah. God was pondering, considering, looking for a messenger. Three facts are amazing. The first is that there was such a problem for God. Surely He had no difficulty in finding someone to take His messages. Were not the seraphim quivering in eager anticipation of His slightest commands? But a word from the Lord of hosts, and in a flash they would speed away to swift obedience. The seraphim, however, lacked the essential qualification for being sent to the people of Israel. Although they could declare God's holiness to sinful people, they had had no sense of being made holy; for they had never sinned. They had no conception of the utter desolation that sweeps over a guilty man standing before God. They covered their faces when waiting before the Lord, but they had never known the desire to flee headlong from His presence, crying, "Woe is me, for I am undone!" Forgiveness and cleansing were experiences they had neither known nor needed.

The second amazing fact is the daring of Isaiah. "Here am I," he said, "send me." One moment he was crying, "Woe is me," and the next he calls out boldly, "Send me." What qualifications did he have to make such an offer? He who had known the shame of sin, and the sweetness of cleansing, was eminently fitted to go to a nation whose people were of unclean lips.

The Bible contains no theories: it is packed with facts. All of those facts are clearly stated, demonstrated, proved, and illustrated. Cleansing from sin and being made holy are not merely doctrines, they are acts of God, and experiences of the people of God. Neither doctrine can be taught without first being experienced, for the Christian is primarily a witness, that is, a person who has personal knowledge of what he is talking about. When the Church shifts from declaring divine truths to speculative theories, she has no message worth uttering, or that will save the world. God's call is for men with cleansed lips to go and tell that through Christ there is cleansing from all sin. His search is for men who have been made holy to go and declare that God can make even a sinner holy through Christ. "Be ye holy for I am holy" not only gives the reason why we should be holy, but also makes clear how we can be holy. Since God is holy, we can become the same. Command and possibility are one. Isaiah could speak of this with the utmost assurance for he had experienced it. "We speak that we do know" must be the testimony of every true servant of God. Without that qualification he has no right to open his mouth in the name of the Lord.

Third, it amazes us that the prophet's offer was accepted. What grace! God did not disqualify him because of past failure. Lips that had once been stained by sin were not silenced forever. God said, "Go and tell" (v. 9). If the first step toward holiness was confession of need, then the first step in the way of holiness was obedience to the command. Isaiah was to enter into the same relationship to God as the seraphim who were committed to instant obedience, hiding themselves and speaking of their Lord alone. Just as the vision of God resulted in no ecstatic experience, but rather an acute awareness of his sin, so cleansing and commissioning did not consist in a kind of warm emotional glow, but rather in a specific, clear call to go and tell other people about the Lord.

Holiness for us will be of the same pattern. God has not changed. The hosts of the angels still surround Him, proclaiming that He is holy. But for the carrying of the good news of cleansing from sin for men and women in need, He still chooses to use those who have confessed their sin and been made holy through faith in the blood of His Son, and by the operation of His own Spirit within them.

# Chapter Three

And it shall come to pass in the day that Jehovah shall give thee rest from thy sorrow, and from thy trouble, and from the hard service wherein thou wast made to serve, that thou shalt take up this parable against the king of Babylon, and say, How hath the oppressor ceased! the golden city ceased! Jehovah hath broken the staff of the wicked, the scepter of the rulers; that smote the peoples in wrath with a continual stroke, that ruled the nations in anger, with a persecution, that none restraineth. The whole earth is at rest, and is quiet; they break forth into singing. Yea, the fir trees rejoice at thee, and the cedars of Lebanon, saying, Since thou art laid low, no hewer is come up against us. Sheol from beneath is moved for thee to meet thee at thy coming; it stirreth up the dead for thee, even all the chief ones of the earth; it hath raised up from their thrones all the kings of the nations. All they shall answer and say unto thee, Art thou also become weak as we? art thou become like unto us? Thy pomp is brought down to Sheol, and the noise of thy voice: the worm is spread under thee, and worms cover thee.

How art thou fallen from heaven, O day-star, son of the morning! how are thou cut down to the ground, that didst lay low the nations! And thou saidst in thy heart, I will ascend into heaven, I will exalt my throne above the stars of God; and I will sit upon the mount of congregation, in the uttermost parts of the north; I will ascend above the heights of the clouds; I will make myself like the Most High. Yet thou shalt be brought down to Sheol, to the uttermost parts of the pit. They that see thee shall gaze at thee, they shall consider thee, saying, Is this the man that made the earth to tremble, that did shake kingdoms; that made the world as a wilderness, and overthrew the cities thereof; that let not loose his prisoners to their home? All the kings of the nations, all of *them, sleep in glory, everyone in his own house. But thou art cast forth away from thy sepulcher like an abominable branch, clothed with the slain, that are thrust through with the sword, that go down to the stones of the pit; as a dead body trodden under foot. Thou shalt not be joined with them in burial, because thou hast destroyed thy land, thou hast slain thy people; the seed of evildoers shall not be named forever....*

*Jehovah of hosts hath sworn, saying, Surely, as I have thought, so shall it come to pass; and as I have purposed, so shall it stand: that I will break the Assyrian in my land, and upon my mountains tread him under foot: then shall his yoke depart from off them, and his burden depart from off their shoulder.*

-Isaiah 14:3-20, 24, 25

# CHRIST, LORD OVER THE DEVIL

---

GOD IS NOT AT WAR WITH MAN, and, in the beginning, the idea of making war on God never occurred to man. In fact, neither Adam nor any of his descendants had any reason for rebelling against their Creator, but had the fancy ever been entertained of challenging God, it must have been immediately obvious that no man could have survived for a moment such an unequal match. The fantastic idea of rising in revolt was injected into Adam's mind by Satan who had himself tried the dangerous experiment with disastrous results. In his bitter mind evolved the dark and dreadful strategy of turning men against the One who loved them best. From his first intrusion into our history, the Devil has been a determined, ruthless rival of our Lord

Jesus Christ; and God, with a wisdom that defies our understanding, has tolerated the fierce resistance of the depraved prince that He once created as a creature of great intelligence and power. Satan is determined that Christ shall never be acknowledged openly as Lord. God has irrevocably declared that His Son shall be universally reverenced as Lord. All worldly struggles are an outcome of that major, terrible conflict. Man's heart is the battlefield. In Isaiah 14 we find a graphic unveiling of the nature and end of the strange being who dared to challenge God and whose energies are bent toward turning man against his Lord.

In its historic setting, the passage unquestionably refers to the king of Babylon. A careful reading of verses 4 through 23 will make that clear. Isaiah is commanded to "take up this proverb against the king of Babylon," and in the closing verses of the section we read: "For I will rise up against them, saith the Lord of hosts, and cut off from Babylon the name, and remnant, and son, and nephew, saith the Lord" (14:22). The Bible, however, is not merely an accurate historical record of ancient matters: it is a book of principles. To ignore the historical background, or to violate the grammar of Scripture may easily lead to a false understanding or to ridiculous interpretations, but historical research and grammatical analyses are no more than a means to the ultimate objective of discovering the basic principles that God has revealed in His holy Word. In this particular chapter, the historical background is Babylon. As to grammar, the subject of the whole passage from verse 4 through verse 23 remains unchanged, and yet, in verse 12, the new name of Lucifer suddenly appears. Some expositors would have us believe that the reference is still to the king of Babylon. Others, including many of the Church Fathers and such later writers as

Luther, see in the name a reference to the Devil. In principle, the passage may apply equally to king and Devil. A change of reference from the king of Babylon to the prince of darkness is neither abrupt nor inappropriate since the former was the agent of the latter. In manner of life, habits of speech, and ultimate end Babylon's ruler is strikingly similar to Satan himself. The king is a chip off the old block! The principles by which these two live their lives are identical, and the chapter may be applied prophetically to Satan, or historically to his puppet who ruled over the Babylonian Empire. Two basic truths emerge from these twenty verses: self-exaltation is the essence of evil, and self-exaltation leads to Hell.

Satan was the real power behind the scenes: the Babylonian monarch was no more than a cooperating agent. Satan was the mastermind for the ambitious lust for power and the ruthless cruelty of the king who ignorantly obeyed the will of his unseen lord. Man's choice lies between two extremes. Sinning, he can do the will of the Devil; fulfilling righteousness, he can do the will of God. Every action, thought, word and purpose falls into one of those two categories. Heaven or Hell approves all we say, think, and do. Men either unconsciously and ignorantly obey Satan, or consciously and willingly obey the Lord. Either we are the blind, shackled slaves of Satan or we are the freewill bondmen of Jesus Christ. Every man has a master, satanic or divine, and each has a master of his own choice.

The king of Babylon, then, was a servant whose character faithfully reproduced that of his lord, and the story makes an easy transfer from slave to master at verse 12: "O Lucifer, son of the morning!" The name is suggestive. It could equally well be translated, "Thou star of light, sun of dawn." The reference is to the bright, morning star, and the name properly belongs to Christ. In the last chapter of the Bible, as our Lord speaks His final words to John, He says: "I am the root and the offspring of David, and the bright and morning star" (Rev. 22:16). Like many another expression in Scripture, this descriptive title is no poetic fancy but figurative language full of meaning. Just as the bright, morning star declares the end of the long dark hours of the night, and heralds the coming of a fresh new day, so Christ appeared amid the black hopelessness of a world away from God to bring promise of a new day of light and life. All the hopes kindled in the hearts of the eastern Wise Men, who saw His star in the East, were more than fulfilled by His actual appearing. From that time, Christ's coming into the world and into the hearts of countless millions of people was to be like the blazing appearance of a star brighter than the dawn. This title, then, that so well described the Saviour, appealed to the Evil One whose ambition was to appear before men in a dazzling glory that would hide his real nature. But his speech betrayed him.

Language reveals character, especially the use of pronouns. The Devil's vocabulary is generously sprinkled with the pronoun I. The king of Babylon talked in exactly the same way. Count the personal pronouns in 14:13, 14 and you will find that the Devil refers to himself five times. "I will ascend ... I will exalt ... I will sit ... I will ascend ... I will make myself." When Satan tempted Christ, his language bore the same characteristic. "All this power will I give thee, and the glory of them: for that is delivered unto me; and to whomsoever I will I give it. If thou therefore wilt worship me, all shall be thine." Five times in one short sentence he speaks of himself In striking contrast, our Lord Jesus in His replies to the Tempter never once used the pronoun I.

46

This self-centered language reveals the essence of evil. Sin is the government of self by self for self: the sinner is egocentric and his language reveals it. In religious discussions, the non-Christian view is usually prefaced with such expressions as, In my opinion"; "I mean to say"; or "If you ask me, I think." Every man has the right to have his own opinions, but opinions stubbornly held against the revealed will of God are sin.

In one of the great Japanese universities where we used to meet weekly for Bible study, a student asked for a definition of sin. Like most of the others in the group he was an extremely intelligent young man familiar with the ancient and modem philosophies of East and West. Socrates, Plato, Kant, Russell, Dewey, and Sartre were names that fell easily from his lips. He had recently attended a conference at which a learned professor of theology had lectured with great erudition on the subject of sin, liberally interlacing his discourse with quotations in Greek, Hebrew, German, and English. But scholastic fireworks had merely dazzled the student without answering his question. Like Nehemiah, "I prayed to the God of heaven" for a clear and simple answer. The members of the class were all students of English literature and from one of the first lessons in English grammar came the answer. First person singular: *I*; second person: *You*; third person: *He*. I, you, he—that is sin. Myself first, other people second, and God last. Reverse the order, and we have righteousness. He, God, first; you, my neighbor, second; and I, myself, in the last place. The language of the Pharisee at his devotions perfectly illustrates that sin is self-obsession. "I thank thee, that I am not as the rest of men.... I fast twice in the week; I give tithes of all that I get." His fasting and faithful tithing had divine sanction, and yet they were done in the absurd conceit that he was not as other men. Like the Devil himself, in one short sentence optimistically put together as a prayer, the Pharisee used the pronoun *I* five times. In sin, plans, hopes, ideas and everything else originate with self, and are for the benefit of self. Even what appears to be good is, in fact, what we ourselves consider to be good for ourselves, and should the action by chance indeed be good, then the motive may easily be our self-satisfaction, or the bolstering of self-conceit.

Self-exaltation knows no limits. We have already discovered the Devil's favorite pronoun. Now look at his verbs in those same two verses: "ascend ... exalt ... sit ... ascend ... make." Every word expresses his insatiable ambition to climb higher and yet higher.

"I will ascend into heaven." No place is considered too good for him. No matter whether we regard the king of Babylon or the Devil as the speaker, it is equally fantastic that either of them should seriously talk as if going to Heaven merely depended on his own decision. The problem of ascending to Heaven is not just the question of space travel. Even if man one day stands triumphant—and cold—upon the moon*, he will still be as far from Heaven as he was before be set out. Ascending to Heaven is a moral problem, not a geographical challenge. "Naught that defileth shall ever enter in." Such a consideration never occurred to the Devil or his earthly representative. Self-exaltation sees no difficulty at all in getting to Heaven. Millions cherish the strange fantasy that they can do as they please, even to the extent of totally ignoring God's will, and then blithely decide to soar peacefully from their death-beds to a blissful Heaven. An earthworm might as well

---

* Neil Armstrong set "his foot" on the moon on July 20, 1969.

dream rosy dreams of flying to the moon.

"I will exalt my throne above the stars of God." In those words the fixed purpose of Satan is plainly declared. He is perhaps not very good at keeping secrets. Like all egotists, he has difficulty in keeping to himself his big plans for himself. The Devil wants a throne. He seeks a throne in every human heart: he covets a throne over all mankind. But above all else, he wants *the* throne, the throne that is above every throne. He will be satisfied with nothing less than absolute authority. The empire he has in mind not only includes this world, but the whole universe. His objective is a throne "above the stars of God." Whether "stars" are understood literally or as symbolic of heavenly powers makes no difference. Satan wants to be above everybody and over everything. His quest is not for an empty title, or tinsel glory but for effective control of all that exists.

His stupendous pride and colossal ambition may be perverted relics of his former high estate as one of the greatest of the angels. In his fallen condition, lust for his lost powers drives him on relentlessly like a frenzied madman casting himself in the role of an Alexander the Great. Once the Devil possessed power for the glory of God; now he desires power for his own glory. Heaven is not too good for him, and no place too high for his throne. More than even all this, Satan seeks universal worship and has plainly said so. Once he starts his boasting, he has difficulty in getting his mouth shut. "I will sit on the mount of the assembly in the far north" (14:13). The Babylonians believed that their gods lived in the cloudy mountain peaks to the north of their country. This further declaration of the Devil, therefore, reveals that he would not only ascend to the holy courts of Heaven where God is worshiped, but that he would also claim a prominent seat among the gods of the heathen. His dual quest is for power and worship. About 800 years after the time of Isaiah, in tempting Christ, the Devil once more laid bare the secret of his heart by offering the Lord Jesus all the kingdoms of the world, including their material glory, in exchange for one act of worship. "All this will I give thee if thou wilt worship me."

But his ambition has not yet reached its climax. He would go higher. "I will ascend above the heights of the clouds" (14:14). He desires position. The reference may be either to clouds above the dwelling place of the Babylonian gods or to angels of God, who are sometimes referred to in this symbolic manner. In either case, the meaning is identical. Satan wants the highest possible position above all supernatural creatures, whether real or imaginary. He would be above the God whom men ought to worship, and above the gods that men in fact do worship. He seeks to surpass in splendor Michael and Gabriel, the mighty archangels, and to excel the seraphim surrounding God's throne, and all the cherubim and countless holy angels.

Finally the Devil's audacity reaches its incredible climax. "I will make myself like the Most High" (14-14). Now his plan is complete. He would usurp God, sit upon the throne of absolute authority and receive the adoration of all creation. That is, he would possess the position of glory and honor which is reserved for Christ Jesus. The Devil stands unmasked as the proud rival of the Lord of hosts Himself.

Pride is a kind of madness. Obadiah uncovers the heart of the matter when he says of Edom, "The pride of thine heart hath deceived thee." Pride is self-deceit. Pride never deceives God; seldom deceives men, for the haughty man is easily recognizable, but pride always deceives the man himself. The king of Babylon and the prince of darkness are alike in that both dreamed the dreams of self-deceived fools. Imagine that man or demon should ever indulge in the reverie of replacing God! But men have had that notion. In older times, world conquerors such as the great Caesar, Alexander, and Kublai Khan dreamed dreams of empires that had but little room for God, and in modern history blasphemous dictators such as Stalin have claimed to have successfully ousted God. In our day we are seeing the Devil's supreme effort to weld the world into one kingdom in preparation for the day when he will produce his direct representative to rule all mankind. Then will appear the modern counterpart of the king of Babylon, repeating the same egotistic language first heard in the days of Isaiah.

Not only devils and dictators talk this way. Modern man follows the same pattern. Scientific developments and new methods in education have produced a spirit of confidence in which man is sure that he can make himself whatever he pleases. Revolutionary discoveries, brilliant techniques, and an increasing mastery over nature have persuaded men of the twentieth century that, given time, they can do anything. A perverted form of Christianity has encouraged that belief. One of the tragic results of trying to adjust the Gospel to modern ideas has been to credit man with a kind of divinity that ill fits his actual character. By making Christ less than Deity and making man almost divine, misguided theologians have reduced the difference between God and man to so little that it no longer appears to matter. And man cries in triumph, "I will make myself like the Most High."

The theory that an artful and ambitious little amoeba once planned for itself a great future which would reach a triumphant climax in man, who in turn would be able to invent the ambitious little amoeba as his ancestor, may be less acceptable now than a generation ago, but the concept that man is a self-made creature dies hard. Sections of the church subscribed to this view, and hastened to reiterate the doctrine of the dignity of human personality. Experimentally-minded scientists and woolly-minded theologians together invented a little hero called Modern Man who, by some strange trick, had escaped all the contamination of the sins of his forefathers—if he had any. This new type Man was presented as a creature of infinite worth, unlimited powers, but with no future. Nothing was needed but to develop the miracle personality within this creature of infinite possibilities. So self-sufficient had man become that God seemed unnecessary, either scientifically or theologically. Man was everything. To very few did it occur that this masterpiece was a creation of the Devil and not of the philosopher or scientist. Many failed to recognize the language of the Devil boastfully repeated in an age that has almost written off the Devil as an anachronism.

Sin, then, is more than breaking the law of God: it is becoming like the Devil. A metamorphosis is taking place in every heart. Either we are being "conformed to the image of his Son," or we are being remorselessly changed into the likeness of Satan himself. The choice is our own.

All who reject Christ and tacitly acquiesce in the rule of the prince of the power of the air seldom stop to consider what would happen if the Devil were successful in his plot to overthrow the throne of God. Evidently he was confident of victory or he would never have made the attempt. Many of the angels were dazzled by the brilliance of his plans and persuaded of his ability. They followed him in high hopes of glory. Satan's vast organization, prodigious efforts, and subtle planning are all based on the supposition that triumph is not only possible but probable. His language shows no trace of lack of confidence. And his high percentage of success in mastering the minds and ruining the lives of millions of men and women bolster his self-assurance.

By the Devil's past achievements we may accurately judge what would happen if he ruled the universe. On his arrival in Hell, he is greeted with astonishment by those who recall his former reputation. "Is this the man that made the earth to tremble, and did shake kingdoms; that made the world as a wilderness, and overthrow the cities thereof; that let not loose the prisoners to their homes?" (14:16, 17). Fear, chaos, barrenness, destruction, and captivity—these are the works of the Devil. His kingdom is a rule of fear. Terror would rule on high if Satan grasped the power to reign. He has injected this very idea into the vacuous minds of those who have rejected God. When the leaders of the Soviet Union and other pagan communistic states denied that Jesus is Lord they became an easy prey for the Evil One who holds exactly the same views. Into such hands he places a scepter of fear by which they now control the minds and bodies of half the world. Communist countries are grim evidence that where the Devil reigns, fear is rampant. "He makes the earth to tremble."

Next, like a sadistic ogre, amusing himself with hapless little creatures in his relentless grasp, Satan shakes the kingdoms. He is the great disturber of the peace. Within this century, world maps have been redrawn constantly as new convulsions have altered national boundaries. This historic kaleidoscope is the Devil's work. Inflaming passions and instilling pride as arrogant as his own, he incites nation against nation. He delights in unsettled conditions, rejoices in restlessness, and encourages feverish activity lest men and women should have time to think of God. Shaking kingdoms, tottering empires and chaotic conditions are ideal for his purposes. If he were to rule over all, universal restlessness and general instability would persist forever.

To fear and chaos Satan adds destruction. He "makes the world as a wilderness." The Devil hates life because life is from God. Wherever he has trodden, the earth has been scorched by his footprint. This truth holds literally as well as spiritually. The great deserts, treeless and trackless, without grass or flowers, became that way through war, neglect, or ignorance of the laws of God. God "makes the desert blossom as a rose," but His great enemy would turn every Paradise into a barren wilderness if he had the opportunity. In the human heart Satan blasts away until the holy ambitions and fair dreams of youth are dried up, and noble resolutions and high hopes of later years are parched. Only a miniature Sahara remains.

"He destroyed the cities thereof" (14:17). Satan smashes everything he touches. His intent is to ruin all that God has made. Cities are his special target, for in the destruction of a crowded city the Devil reaps a swift and terrible harvest of souls. The material damage caused by the falling of an atomic bomb on Hiroshima was negligible compared with the spiritual tragedy that swiftly swept thousands into a dark eternity.

If an observer from another planet were to visit this world and, after watching the laborious efforts of millions of people to create large and splendid cities, see the citizens turn with great ferocity on each other and smash to pieces their own achievements, he would then conclude either that men are mad, or that we are under the control of some evil influence. Both conclusions would be true. The Devil is the unseen destroyer, and men are mad to obey him. If Satan were to rule the universe, destruction would be his practice. Not only would cities be laid in ruins, but faith, hope, love, joy, and peace, and every good gift that God ever made would be taken from the face of the earth.

Finally, he "let not loose his prisoners to their home" (14:17). Of his own will, Satan never lets go a single captive. On human level, escape is an absolute impossibility. The doors of his jail are tightly shut, and no matter how much men may delude themselves, they are no freer than a bird whose only liberty is to fly frantically within the narrow limits of its little cage. Proof is easy. Name any evil habit of which you are conscious, and then try to struggle free of your own unaided efforts. Make an effort to liberate yourself from every entanglement of evil in thought, word, deed, or motive, and you will find escape impossible. If the Devil succeeded in his plans, all men would be slaves. Indeed, men are already slaves where his power is operative. The Gospel and freedom are concomitants: the Devil's power and slavery are inseparable. Satanically inspired Communism strikingly demonstrates slavery of a new kind in which mind and spirit, as well as body, are shackled with the iron chains of Hell.

If Satan were to gain a complete victory, he would completely reverse the work of God. His kingdom would be characterized by fear, instability, and destruction. His empire would be a desert in which unhappy, hopeless prisoners would drag out eternal years of misery.

"How art thou fallen from heaven, 0 Lucifer son of the morning! how art thou cut down to the ground"

(14:12). Hallelujah! Even the mechanical process of typing these words cannot quench the exhilaration of spirit surging up at the discovery that Satan cannot succeed. The lordship of the Devil is not a pleasant prospect, and God's mighty oath that the enemy shall fail is a needed reassurance.

"Jehovah of hosts hath sworn, saying, Surely, as I have thought, so shall it come to pass; and, as I have purposed so shall it stand: that I will break the Assyrian" (14:24, 25). The words have no great importance to us of the twentieth century if their meaning is limited only to an ancient emperor, but God's intentions are identical whether for the king of Babylon, the Assyrian Empire, later generations of sinful egotists, or the Devil himself. The eternal pattern for dealing with pride is starkly clear in a divine comment on a human boast. "Thou saidst in thy heart, I will ascend into heaven" (14:13)—that is the human boast. "How art thou fallen from heaven!" (14:12)—that is the divine comment.

In his battle for the throne of God, Satan has suffered a series of resounding defeats. His initial onslaught met with swift retaliation as he was ignominiously hurled from Heaven. The Lord's victory over the Devil is being worked out more slowly on earth. The birth of Christ at Bethlehem was invasion of the enemy's territory. Christ's life was victory over Satan on a human level. For more than thirty-three years, our Saviour consistently defeated the enemy in every form of spiritual combat and under every circumstance that man could know. In boyhood and manhood, at home and in public, in thought and life, in word and deed, Jesus daily lived in constant triumph over the Devil. As God, He could not be tempted, for "God cannot be tempted with evil" (James 1:13), but as Son of man he was "in all points tempted like as we are," and overcame through the same powers available to all believers. If Christ had used divine powers to resist Satan, then He would have destroyed him by the breath of His nostrils or cast him headlong into Hell, but instead He chose to overcome by the fullness of the Holy Spirit, and a confident use of the Word of God. But neither the birth nor the life of Christ was His greatest triumph. That was gained at the cross. That was the critical battle. His strategy was to stoop so low that He seemed to be at the mercy of evil men and their more evil master. Whenever did the Lord of hosts appear more helpless than when He hung limp and lifeless on a cross, His hands and feet transfixed by Roman nails? If ever the halls of Hell resounded with confident, leering laughter, it was that day. But the echoes had scarcely died in those dark, forbidding caverns when all Heaven thundered with mighty hallelujahs as the Lord came forth from His rocky grave, like a shining, splendid knight newly victorious from mortal combat with a fearful foe. "He is risen!" He was bruised, of course, by battle, but Satan's proud head received a fatal wound from which he can never recover. It may be that the once brilliant mind of Satan was so damaged then that he can no longer understand the plans of God and must remain in ignorance of his own eternal fate. What is certain is that the enemy was routed, and all his plans destined to fail.

Hell, not Heaven, is his final abode—his only kingdom a shadowy land of darkness. Instead of the adoration of the universe, the astonishment of Hell awaits him. "Sheol from beneath is moved for thee to meet thee at thy coming; it stirreth up the dead for thee, even all the chief ones of the earth; it hath raised up from their thrones all the kings of the nations" (14:9). At Satan's appearance, kings rise from phantom thrones to welcome the distinguished arrival. Rulers of forgotten empires, once-powerful kings of glittering Babylon, Assyrian rulers of faded magnificence, Egyptian Pharaohs and Roman Caesars, together with the self-inflated Alexanders, Napoleons, Hitlers, Stalins, and other lesser despots, each ambitious for himself in his own peculiar way, all united in a denial that Christ is Lord, and each with a heart in which the frustration of unsatisfied desire alternates with despairing remorse—these, all of these, rise from tawdry thrones, aghast to find that their master is no conquering hero but a beaten, battered broken Devil. The incredible has come to pass! He who boasted that he would storm Heaven and overthrow the throne of God, finds himself languishing upon a bed of worms. He ends his career naked and feeble, defeated and stripped of all he ever had. Hell re-echoes with the despairing, astonished cry of the assembled multitude: "Art thou also become weak as we? Art thou become like unto us?" (14:10). Where are those promises? Where are those boasts? Where is the throne?

Heaven and Hell are the great realities. Death is the door to enlightenment. In Hell, men see the Devil as he is and the consequences of acquiescing to his rule. In Heaven we shall see Christ as He is, and the consequences of accepting Him as Lord. In Hell men see exactly what they have chosen and what they have lost. In Heaven we shall discover the realities of life and light, and know Him whom "having not seen we love." Hell will be filled with the weeping, wailing, and gnashing of teeth of sinners who discover their own bankruptcy. Hell is where men and women at last awake to the fact that they have been deceived by specious promises of Satan, and chased the mirage of self-exaltation.

God in grace has revealed these future conditions to us that we might be warned, and wisely choose His way. This chapter, regardless of how we interpret its chief characters, teaches the never-to-be-forgotten truth that self-exaltation leads to Hell. The king of Babylon went that way. Million of others have followed him. The Devil leads.

Before we turn to another chapter of Isaiah, let us reduce this subject to its simplest elements. Jesus will conquer because He has already conquered. Satan will be defeated because he has already been decisively beaten. Jesus is Lord over the Devil and all powers of darkness. Between these two, Jesus and Satan, each of us must make a choice, and that choice leads upward to the glory of Heaven, or down to the despair of Hell.

# Chapter Four

Now it came to pass in the fourteenth year of king Hezekiah, that Sennacherib king of Assyria came up against all the fortified cities of Judah, and took them. And the king of Assyria sent Rabshakeh from Lachish to Jerusalem unto king Hezekiah with a great army, And he stood by the conduit of the upper pool in the highway of the fuller's field....

And Rabshakeh said unto them, Say ye now to Hezekiah, Thus saith the great king, the king of Assyria, What confidence is this wherein thou trusteth? I say, thy counsel and strength for the war are but vain words: now on whom dost thou trust, that thou hast rebelled against me? Behold, thou trustest upon the staff of this bruised reed, even upon Egypt, whereon if a man lean, it will go into his hand, and pierce it: so is Pharaoh king of Egypt to all that trust on him. But if thou say unto me, We trust in Jehovah our God: is not that he, whose high places and whose altars Hezekiah hath taken away, and hath said to Judah and to Jerusalem, Ye shall worship before this altar? ...

Then Rabshakeh stood, and cried with a loud voice in the Jews' language, and said, Hear ye the words of the great king, the king of Assyria. Thus saith the king, Let not Hezekiah deceive you; for he will not be able to deliver you: neither let Hezekiah make you trust in Jehovah, saying, Jehovah will surely deliver us; this city shall not be given into the hand of the king of Assyria. Hearken not to Hezekiah: for thus saith the king of Assyria, Make your peace with me, and come out to me; and eat ye every one of his vine, and every one of his fig tree, and drink ye everyone the waters of his own cistern; until I come and take you away to a land like your own land, a land of grain and new wine, a land of bread and vineyards....

But they held their peace, and answered him not a word; for the king's commandment was, saying, Answer him not.

And it came to pass, when king Hezekiah heard it, that

*he rent his clothes, and covered himself with sack cloth, and went into the house of Jehovah. And he sent Eliakim, who was over the household, and Shebna the scribe, and the elders of the priests, covered with sackcloth, unto Isaiah the prophet the son of Amoz.... So the servants of king Hezekiah came to Isaiah.... So Rabshakeh returned, and found the king of Assyria warring against Libnah; for he had heard that he was departed from Lachish. And he heard say concerning Tirhakah king of Ethiopia, He is come out to fight against thee. And when he heard it, he sent messengers to Hezekiah, saying, Thus shall ye speak to Hezekiah king of Judah, saying, Let not thy God in whom thou trusteth deceive thee, saying, Jerusalem shall not be given into the hand of the king of Assyria. . . . And Hezekiah received the letter from the hand of the messengers, and read it; and Hezekiah went up unto the house of Jehovah, and spread it before Jehovah.... Then Isaiah the son of Amoz sent unto Hezekiah, saying, Thus saith Jehovah, the God of Israel, Whereas thou hast prayed to me against Sennacherib king of Assyria, this is the word which Jehovah hath spoken concerning him: The virgin daughter of Zion hath despised thee and laughed thee to scorn; the daughter of Jerusalem hath shaken her head at thee. Whom hast thou defied and blasphemed? and against whom hast thou exalted thy voice and lifted up thine eyes on high? even against the Holy One of Israel....*

*And the angel of Jehovah went forth, and smote in the camp of the Assyrians a hundred and fourscore and five thousand; and when men arose early in the morning, behold, these were all dead bodies. So Sennacherib king of Assyria departed, and went and returned, and dwelt at Nineveh. And it came to pass, as he was worshiping in the house of Nisroch his god, that Adrammelech and Sharezer his sons smote him with the sword; and they escaped into the land of Ararat. And Esarhaddon his son reigned in his stead.*

—Isaiah 36: 1, 2, 4-7, 13-17, 21; 37:1, 2, 5, 8-10, 14, 21-23, 36-38

# CHRIST THE LORD
# OF VICTORY

"SENNACHERIB King of Assyria came up against all the fortified cities of Judah, and took them" (36:1). Bible history is not simply a true record of events, but a revelation of basic principles involved in the events. Just as the character of the king of Babylon in chapter 14 accurately mirrors the character of the Devil, so the methods of the king of Assyria in this chapter reveal the common methods of Satan in attacking the believer. We have an opportunity to watch the enemy in action

His first onslaught was against the garrison towns guarding the boundaries of Judah. Small victories over small cities were a prelude to the main drive of the capital. The first objective was to neutralize the outer defenses: the ultimate aim was the occupation of the citadel of Jerusalem.

This is the standard operational procedure with the enemy. He is bent upon enslaving the Christian in heart, mind, and will, but his first attacks are rarely a bold frontal move. He plans the final, catastrophic collapse through a long series of minor defeats that soften resistance to the fierce, climactic temptation. The sudden downfall of a Christian is never unexpected by Satan. He has been carefully scheming for it. He first moved against the perimeter defense of daily prayer and Bible study, and gained an astonishingly easy victory. Personal devotions become the exception rather than the rule. He then directed his forces against the fortified city of fellowship with other Christians, knowing that his victim would be much more vulnerable if he could be isolated. Having overcome two defense bastions without much trouble, Satan then probed the Christian's defenses with small temptations. He alerted his forces at times when the believer was least alert. He found, perhaps, that his still unsuspecting dupe was careless with his eyes, and he proceeded with a plan to ruin him through adultery. The warning of the Lord Jesus that "he that looketh on a woman to lust after her hath committed adultery with her already in his heart" would have saved the child of God at this point, but the garrison town of Bible reading had already been destroyed. And so the enemy moved relentlessly in for the kill. What seemed like the inexplicable moral crash of a strong Christian was, in fact, the predictable defeat of a believer weakened by successive minor defeats inflicted on the perimeter of his life. The "defensed cities" had all been destroyed, and the heart was vulnerable.

The king of Assyria did indeed next appear at the gates of Jerusalem. "And the king of Assyria sent Rabshakeh from Lachish to Jerusalem" (36:2). In the confidence of easy victories already gained, this high ranking officer, with the title of Rabshakeh, boldly strode up to the capital. His methods exactly portray the technique of the Devil in attacking the heart of the Christian.

First he used argument calculated to undermine confidence in God. "And Rabshakeh said unto them, Say ye now to Hezekiah, Thus saith the great king, the king of Assyria, What confidence is this wherein thou trustest?" (36-4). Whenever men have heard subtle suggestions that God is not to be trusted, then that has been the voice of the Devil. The insinuation is always made with the utmost confidence. "On whom dost thou trust, that thou hast rebelled against me?" (36:5). Satan asserts his claims and denies God's faithfulness. With ancient arrogance he suggests that the Christian is slightly confused. To put the old argument in modern style, we can paraphrase the Rabshakeh's message. "You may not realize it of course," says the Devil, "but I am still your lord. It is ridiculous to think that you can successfully resist me. That decision to follow Christ was just an unfortunate mistake, and you certainly can't expect Him to deliver you."

This argument of the Devil, and the original argument of Rabshakeh, were a mixture of truth and lies. Egypt he called a bruised reed (36:6) that would pierce the hand of any man who leaned upon it for strength. The suggestion was that if Hezekiah, or his nation, had any idea of looking westward to Egypt for help, he would be bitterly disappointed. That was true. Egypt's reputation was nowhere very high, for God Himself had used exactly the same words to describe the country. The Devil, then, will usually start with the truth. "You, of course," he will say in his blandest manner, "are a rather weak Christian, and you certainly do not have any of that boldness which Peter, for example, had. And then you are not the strong-willed type, which means that you can't expect much success. You are also inclined to be shy, and scared of making a mistake." Since he has been carefully watching you to find your weakest points, he will have no difficulty in bringing these to your notice with the frank opinion that if you are relying on your own resources, then you are in for trouble. Unhappily, most of what he tells us is true. It may even be altogether true.

To the truth, Satan adds a generous amount of error. "But if thou say unto me, We trust in Jehovah our God: is not that he, whose high places and whose altars Hezekiah hath taken away, and hath said to Judah and to Jerusalem, Ye shall worship before this altar?" (36:7). Even the lie was as near as possible to the truth, for the

Devil likes to talk like a gentleman. Hezekiah certainly had removed high places and altars, but the altars were pagan and the high places profane. What the king had destroyed had not belonged to God, but had been an invention of the Devil himself. The device of the enemy was to misrepresent Hezekiah's action because he knew that perverted truth is more dangerous than an outright lie.

Satan undermines a Christian's faith by subtly suggesting that we have unconsciously displeased the Lord. Dragging out some half-forgotten incident, he accuses us of having so offended the Lord that we can no longer expect help from Him. Either be will dig up some former sin, or he will insist that what we sincerely thought to be the will of God was, in fact, all a big mistake. By persuading us that what we thought was the Lord's will was really misguided zeal, he reduces us to a state of endless worry and general confusion. This is his aim. Satan strongly relies for success on the disorder he creates. Enveloping his victim in a swirling fog of lies, he prepares to suggest that the Christian cannot possibly expect help from God and strives to hide the glorious truth that the Lord never abandons His people. He would have us believe that we can somehow get into a position in which we can no longer expect any help from the Lord.

I remember sitting in the office of an experienced, godly Scottish minister, discussing with him the prospects of going to Japan as a missionary. Behind me were seven hard war years in China. The present held a fruitful ministry which, through the church and by radio, was reaching out to a considerable population in Canada. Before me was an open door to the 90 million restless and unsatisfied people of Japan. The problem was whether to stay home, or face again the seething multitudes of turbulent Asia. The old minister's words of counsel showed how well he understood the enemy's devices. "Whatever you decide to do," he said slowly, "you will be tempted to think that you have made a mistake. If you go to Japan, then the Devil will tell you that you would have had a better ministry here: and if you stay here, then the Devil will tell you that you have disobeyed the Lord by not going to Japan." And so it was. And so it is, for Satan is not interested in giving us good advice now or in the future. His only concern is with our past that he might get us unsettled about our present service, and confused about our future. Above all else, he persists in trying to argue the believer away from a quiet confidence in the Lord.

Arguments were followed by promises. "For thus saith the king of Assyria, Make your peace with me, and come out to me; and eat ye every one of his vine, and every one of his fig tree, and drink ye every one the waters of his own cistern" (36:16). The promise of good living was conditional. "Make your peace with me." This is the original proposal for peaceful coexistence. An armistice with the Devil has its strongest appeal to more mature Christians who are strong enough to resist temptation to vile sins, and yet weak enough to be attracted by the idea of sitting contentedly under the shade of a fig tree, and happily enjoying the comforts of a cistern—or swimming pool! After ten or twenty years of struggling against sin, and battling all kinds of spiritual problems, a Christian may easily begin to feel that the warfare has already gone on long enough. As he looks wearily for a place of refuge from a persistent enemy, he will find himself face to face with his opponent who, smiling ingratiatingly, will suggest an easy way out. "Why exhaust yourself by this incessant struggle against me?" Satan asks, with every appearance of being concerned for our good, "Why not relax? Take it easy and forget all about this spiritual battle. After all, you are only human. Better quit all this striving for holiness. And anyway, I'm not suggesting that you do anything particularly wrong: just settle down and enjoy yourself." Or in language more ancient, "Eat ye every one of his own vine, and every one of his fig tree, and drink ye every one of his own cistern." In other words, he suggests that we can escape the heat of the battle by resigning our commissions in the army of the Lord, and concentrating on our own respectable interests. Many a Christian soldier has turned farmer, and devoted all his energies to looking after his fig tree, vine, and cistern.

Is it not possible to live a quiet Christian life without becoming involved in spiritual warfare? The plain answer is, no. If warfare ceases, it is because we have come to terms with the enemy. The conditions of armistice followed the glowing promises, and were rather like the unpleasant clauses of some insurance policies that are printed in microscopic type. "Until I come and take you away to a land like your own land" (36:17). The Assyrian emissary no doubt uttered the words under his breath, for even he must have seen that slavery was a high price to pay for a few vines and fig trees. And it must be equally obvious that there is no land like Emanuel's land. When this offer of peaceful coexistence is analyzed, we find that its peace is the sullen silence of slavery, and its coexistence no more than a dreary existence with a tyrant as master, in exchange for a life of liberty in Christ. Many, however, have accepted such terms. The Devil transports them by the carload to the Land of Illusion where he drugs them with a powerful soporific to give them the notion that they are serving the Lord by sitting around doing nothing except making sure they themselves are well fed, kind, and comfortable. Some of them, daydreaming beneath their leafy fig trees, even imagine they are soldiers fighting bloody battles for their Lord. And so potent is the wine from their vines that none of them realizes that he has been captured body, mind, and spirit by the Devil. Indeed, he would deeply resent any suggestion that he is no longer an active Christian.

This chapter, however, is not the unmasking of the Devil's successful strategy, but a record of his utter defeat. The tactics are brilliant, but not necessarily invincible. The defenses held against the Assyrians, and the counterattack was gloriously victorious. The defenses were of three kinds: the counterattack in two parts.

"They held their peace, and answered him not a word" (36:21). The blatherings of the Rabshakeh provoked no answer from the silent city walls. His eloquence echoed back unanswered. The Bible does not deal in dramatics, or we would be given a minute, and very amusing, description of the Assyrian officer, surrounded by his admiring staff, finally turning away from the walls of Jerusalem, after exhausting himself with a long speech which apparently had made no impression at all on his audience. Even the most skillful flatterers in his entourage must have found it difficult to persuade their noble lord that he had made the most powerful speech of his life. He had, in fact, done a tremendous job, but he had found that silence is an even more powerful defense.

The wife of a Presbyterian elder once astonished her minister by confessing that she sometimes felt a real bitterness against her husband. A few questions brought to light the cause of the trouble. "When I get mad at him," the lady indignantly explained, "he never says a word, but just sits there quietly in his rocker, smiling at me, and waiting until I calm down. If only he would say something."

Silence may be a sign of strength. Silence is certainly part of our defense against temptation. Any discussion with the Devil is useless and dangerous: useless because be is a "liar from the beginning," and argument with a perjurer is futile and dangerous because any dealings with Satan usually end in defeat. Sit down to discuss a temptation, and you will certainly finish by being convinced that right is wrong. So many of our modern generation have listened to the Devil's plausible arguments to glamorize ancient sins that the words right and wrong have almost lost their meaning. Divorce has become the preparatory step toward a new marriage rather than judgment on a sin punishable by death under the old Jewish law; violence has become part of business procedure; lies have become a useful way of doing things; and we are fast approaching the conditions of ancient Rome where adultery was regarded almost as a social grace. Sin is now merely maladjustment or an unfavorable environment. And the sinner is regarded as a psychiatric patient. Many plausible arguments, presented in scientific jargon, are the modern method of Satan to persuade eager listeners of the twentieth century that sin is no longer sin. Argument with the Devil has produced a generation that is skeptical of all that is good, and gullible of all that is evil. White is now black, and black is now white, as the Devil can easily prove to all who take time to discuss the problem with him. Many a Christian has gone down to defeat through stopping to consider whether what he knew in his heart to be wrong might after all be right. You can never argue with the Devil and win.

The way to victory is silence. Discussion is evidence of weakness. Only those who hope to be defeated will debate the matter with the Enemy. "They held their peace, and answered him not a word; for the king's commandment was, saying, Answer him not." Our King has similar instructions for us.

The second form of defense was fellowship with a man of God. Hezekiah "sent Eliakim, who was over the household, and Shebna the scribe, and the elders of the priests, covered with sackcloth, unto Isaiah the prophet the son of Amoz" (37:2). In the hour of peril, the king turned to the royal counselor who had seen the Lord of hosts, the ultimate end of the enemy, and the littleness of the nations in comparison with God Himself. Hezekiah turned in the direction in which his heart had always been.

The Christian whose insistent independence separates him from the fellowship of other believers will not long survive in the struggle with the powers of darkness. For that reason, the Lord seldom sends out His soldiers on lone patrol. He knows that there are very few whom He can trust to make reconnaissance in enemy territory. As the Enemy is well aware, we are specially vulnerable when we are isolated from other Christians. The converse is also true. Actively united to other believers, we are less likely to fall before the Devil's attacks. None is immune from temptation; none secure against assault. Every warrior has moments of weakness, spasms of fear, and times of uncertainty. God, therefore, would have us a tightly formed unit, together facing the same enemy and the common temptations. Not even the greatest among us can afford to neglect the fellowship of the saints, for every one faces moments of great peril when we need to turn for help to those who are strong. These are God's elite guard, men tried in battle, and who have walked with Him in dangerous places, their very bodies scarred with wounds of honor acquired for the glory of His name.

Until we get the complete account from him in Heaven, we shall never know how much Paul was strengthened by the fellowship of Silas in the prison at Philippi. On his own confession, Paul was a man who knew what it was to be weighed down exceedingly, and to despair even of life. His release from the jail is a thrilling story for us to read and illustrate with our flannelgraph material, but as Paul entered the dark, dirty dungeon, his back torn by the beating and his clothes soaked with blood, he saw nothing to encourage him—and he could not turn to Acts 16 to see how his adventure would end. Satan was attacking, thirsting for revenge after his defeat by the expulsion of an evil spirit from a Philippian girl. Perhaps in the dismal dampness of the cell, the enemy began to suggest to Paul that crossing over from Troas into Europe was all a mistake, and that the vision of a man of Macedonia beseeching him to come over and help was only an illusion. We do not know Paul's thoughts and fears as he sat with Silas in the stocks for the first half of the night. But certainly "about midnight Paul and Silas were praying and singing hymns unto God." Paul alone might have remained in despondent silence. But Silas was there, and perhaps it was he who quietly began humming some early version of "What a Friend We Have in Jesus," until Paul took up the strain and the whole hall was filled with the song, "and the prisoners were listening to them."

Hezekiah needed Isaiah; Paul needed Silas; you need me, and I need you; and we all need each other as we face the perils of temptations and the dangers of the Christian life. When fierce temptation threatens to overwhelm you, refuse to discuss the matter with the Devil, but seek the fellowship of the godliest man you know.

The defenses held. The silent people and their

71

godly king began to see the beginning of victory. The enemy temporarily withdrew from the walls of Jerusalem. The tide of battle was turning, but victory was not yet complete. Easy victory is a delusion, for the enemy will willingly yield an inch in order to gain a yard, and many a Christian has been so exuberated by a small and apparently easy triumph that he has not even noticed the coming of a new onslaught which eventually swept him away. The crisis between Judah and Assyria had not yet been reached.

The Rabshakeh, whose eloquent tongue had failed, then tried with his pen. His threatening letter, delivered by special messengers, began with the astounding challenge: "Let not thy God, in whom thou trustest, deceive thee ... "(37:10) and followed with the bullying boast that no god of any nation had been able to deliver from the might of Assyria. Hezekiah now uses his third form of defense. First there had been a refusal to argue with the enemy; then a seeking for fellowship with a man of God; now comes a committal of the enemy to God in prayer. Once more nothing was said to the enemy, but everything was told to God.

Read slowly that remarkable prayer of the king, and remember that as he knelt in the house of the Lord, with the vitriolic letter spread out for God to read, all the vast forces of a powerful empire were poised to strike at his little country.

The ascription:

> O Jehovah of hosts, the God of Israel
> That sittest above the cherubim,
> Thou art the God, even thou alone,
> Of all the kingdoms of the earth;
> Thou hast made heaven and earth.

72

The first petition:

Incline thine ear, O Jehovah, and hear;
Open thine eyes, O Jehovah and see;
And hear all the words of Sennacherib,
Who hath sent to defy the living God.

The admission:

Of a truth, Jehovah, the kings of Assyria have laid
waste all the countries, and their land, And have
cast their gods into the fire: For they were no gods,
but the work of men's hands, wood and stone;
Therefore they have destroyed them.

The final petition:

Now therefore, O Jehovah our God,
  Save us from his hand,
That all the kingdoms of the earth may know
That thou art Jehovah, even thou only.
                                    —Isaiah 37:16-20

The prayer began with an ascription to the greatness of God. This was no mere piece of fancy eloquence to give the prayer elegance, but it determined what should follow, because prayer can never be bigger than our conception of His greatness. Before Hezekiah could confidently ask his God to deal with the most powerful nation in the world, he had to be sure that he believed that his God was greater than that empire. The king saw Him as Lord of the cherubim, Lord over the nations, and Lord of the whole universe. This was not just a theological proposition, but a fact on which his faith rested. He believed God more than he feared

Assyria.

The first petition reveals the king's full understanding of the nature of the attack. It was defiance of the living God: "Hear all the words of Sennacherib, who hath sent to defy the living God." With rare spiritual insight, he saw that the enemy was not so much concerned with defeating him, as with striking a blow at God Himself. That is the essence of all temptation. It is the Devil mocking God's power. Satan is not particularly concerned with us, for our sake, and he is very little interested in whether we sin or not, except insofar as our behavior reflects on the power and character of God. His challenge is not addressed to us, but to our Lord. "Look at this feeble saint." he jeers. "Do you suppose that God could ever deliver him from my power? Look at all my victories. I defy Him." His threats are hurled about recklessly, and with calculated blasphemy.

When a young Christian, for example, is abruptly severed from his family and church to serve with the Armed Forces overseas, he immediately finds himself surrounded by sinful seductions so strong that the mathematical possibility of his returning home morally unscathed in mind and body is about one in twenty-five. The Devil will not only make sure that temptation is presented in its most glamorous form, but he will also confidently brag that even God cannot keep a man unstained in such a polluted atmosphere. And if he cannot force the Christian into sin, then he will blandly assert that God cannot possibly use one man to witness for Christ in quarters or aboard ship where there is no other believer. Examples and illustrations could be multiplied indefinitely, but the principle remains the same. The Devil defies God to deliver His people. He attacks God through the Christian, which is the only

74

way he can attack God. Deliverance is by referring the whole matter confidently to the Lord. Hezekiah, in effect, prayed, "Hear what the enemy is saying about You, O Lord."

The king frankly admitted that the enemy had had considerable success, but be saw equally clearly that the glittering victories over nations and their pantheon were not due to the greatness of the kings of Assyria, but to the littleness of the gods of the conquered peoples. "They were no gods, but the work of men's hands" (37:19). The prayer that began with a declaration of the greatness of God, and continued with an exposure of the real nature of temptation, now admits that human effort cannot devise a method of countering such an enemy. The world is strewn with the wreckage of schemes that were intended to make men what they ought to be by delivering them from evil influences. Satan has indeed "laid waste all the countries" in spite of profound philosophies, moral codes, new methods of education, and every conceivable variety of religious system. The reason for defeat is evident: the gods were human inventions. There are no gimmicks to give victory over evil. No magic formula, and not even a verse of Scripture used as a kind of lucky charm, will preserve us from the pollution of sin. Deliverance is from God, the living God, alone.

Hezekiah knew that, and realized with crystal clarity the basic reason why God delivers those who call on Him. "Save us from his hand, that all the kingdoms of the earth may know that thou art Jehovah, even thou only" (37:20). The final answer to the defiance of the Devil is the deliverance of the Lord who deals with the temptation for His own sake. God is concerned that His people should be victorious over a mocking enemy, because His own honor is involved, and every temptation is an opportunity for Him to show that He can do what no other can.

The counterattack against the Assyrians was in two parts. First was the answer of Israel (37:22) given her by the Lord; second, was the answer of the Lord (37:23-38). Israel's answer was the laughter of confident faith. "The virgin daughter of Zion hath despised thee and laughed thee to scorn; the daughter of Jerusalem hath shaken her head at thee." What a dramatic picture this is. Sennacherib, conqueror of nations, head of a mighty empire and commander of the most powerful army of the day, laughed at by a girl. It is as if a dainty maiden, leaning over the ramparts of the city to take a look at the massed military might of the greatest nation on earth, should shake her head with uncontrollable mirth at the sight of the powerless hoards. She laughs in scorn at the incredibly silly idea that armed forces should attack the Holy One of Israel, and she despises any who think that God can be defeated.

See it that way, and you also will laugh the laugh of faith. Much of our uncertainty about the outcome of a particular temptation originates in matching our strength against the Devil's, and predicting the result according to whether we are optimistic or pessimistic about ourselves at the time. The way to victory is to be wholly pessimistic about ourselves, and completely optimistic about the Lord. Defeat is born of doubt about God, or confidence in ourselves; victory begins with a conviction that the Lord is capable of dealing with the enemy. That is to say, we take our stand on the basic truth that the Devil is not too strong for the Lord, and that we are not too weak for Him. If the virgin daughter of Zion could dare to scorn the enemy in the name of the Lord, then every child of God has the right to smile at the very idea that Satan could ever defeat the

Lord even in his particular case.

This is no invitation to recklessness or lighthearted jests about the most terrible of all foes, nor does this mean that the proper precautions can be neglected. He who belittles the power of the enemy stands in the greatest of perils, but the Christian who refuses to treat with the Devil, and strengthened by fellowship with the whole household of faith, confidently submits the temptation to God in prayer, can get up from his knees to go out with smiling confidence to meet the foe, knowing full well that the Lord of hosts will Himself enforce a victory. When we are sure of our own great conquering Lord, then we can expect deliverance and triumph even before the battle is joined.

The answer of the Lord was sudden, dramatic, and terrible. As soon as Hezekiah turned the enemy over to God, the Lord immediately took full responsibility for dealing with him, and commenced operations by fixing a hook in his nose. "Because of thy raging against me, and because thine arrogancy is come up into mine ears, therefore will I put my hook in thy nose, and my bridle in thy lips, and I will turn thee back by the way which thou camest" (37:29). Hezekiah had prayed that God would open His ears to hear the defiant words of Sennacherib, and God had promptly answered by listening to the arrogant boasting of the proud ruler which the Lord compared with a lumbering beast to be dragged back by its snout to its lair. Ignominious defeat was about to come for the foe, and a glorious deliverance for Israel. "He shall not come unto this city, nor shoot an arrow there, neither shall he come before it with shield, nor cast up a mound against it" (37:33). Far from destroying the city as he threatened, the enemy would not be able to hit it even with one arrow. That is the kind of deliverance which the Lord has for

77

His people. He has no thought of the kind of victory that is complacently satisfied because enemy sniping failed to keep us from meeting the Lord in prayer twenty-nine days of the month, and only hit us on one day of the thirty. God has no plan of deliverance which provides for a Christian yielding in thought to the temptation, but resisting the urge to put the thought into action. His promise is that the shield of faith is able to quench all the fiery darts of the evil one (Eph. 6:16). When He delivers, the believer is altogether unscathed.

And now comes the kill. First the Assyrians, and then their king, feel the terrible power of the God they have defied. "And the angel of Jehovah went forth, and smote in the camp of the Assyrians a hundred and fourscore and five thousand" (37:36). The Lord of hosts did not summon His hosts; the seraphim were not required to leave their places before the throne; one angel was sufficient to destroy all the fighting men of an entire army.

Some might, and do, object to this bloodthirsty account and suggest that Israel conceived of God as a kind of tribal deity or God of war who gave victory to those who appeased Him. Nothing could be farther from the truth. The Assyrians were fighting men whose business was war, plunder, pillage, and rape. Their boast had been that what they had done to Haran, Gozan, Rezeph, and the children of Eden, they would do to Jerusalem. In waging a war of aggression they faced the normal perils of death and wounds in battle.

There is, however, a deeper truth. The struggle against sin is a war to the death, and in which compromise is impossible. We slay, or are slain; sin destroys us, or we destroy it. The enemy is relentless, cruel, and pitiless, and destruction is his business. And the only method effective against him is a sword.

Silence before the enemy, fellowship with a man of God, prayer and faith led Israel to the miraculous resources of God. "The angel of the Lord went forth." He was not an angel, but the angel who brought deliverance. The first place this angel is referred to in Scripture is in Genesis 22:11 which records Abraham's offering of Isaac. "And the angel of Jehovah called unto him out of heaven, and said, Abraham, Abraham: and he said, Here am I. And he said, Lay not thy hand upon the lad, neither do thou anything unto him; for now I know that thou fearest God, seeing thou hast not withheld thy son, thine only son, from me." The speaker seems to identify God with himself, and the implication is strong that the angel of the Lord is a title for the Lord Himself. The same suggestion is here in Isaiah. The Lord promised, "I will defend this city" (37: 35), and the following verse declares that "the angel of Jehovah went forth." On this point we cannot be certain, but beyond all argument, the final deliverance of Israel and the utter defeat of the enemy was by a miracle for which God was responsible.

In the battle against sin, then, it is the intervention of the Lord that is decisive. The climax comes when God matches His overwhelming powers against the formidable strength of the Devil, and in spite of our pitiful weaknesses, brings off a miraculous victory. If we ever become so desperate that we feel that only a miracle can set us free from Satan's domination, then we have reached the very point at which God is ready to work. And the full miracle is that Christ's unqualified victory over the principalities and powers of darkness at the cross can become our experience through faith in our Lord of hosts whose specialty is miracles.

The victory was complete. Not only was Jerusalem delivered and the Assyrian army annihilated, but their king met with disaster in the presence of his own god. Sennacherib, who had set out as the confident commander of his trusted legions, withdrew from the field of death in the lonely shame of defeat to seek consolation, and perhaps new guidance, by the worship of his god Nisroch in the temple in Nineveh. The sightless eyes and mute tongue of the idol could not warn him of his sons' creeping in stealthily to murder him, and the king who had defied the God of Israel and boasted of his conquests over the gods of Hamath and Arpad was slain, to end his proud career as a lifeless corpse, prostrate before the only object in the world he regarded as greater than himself.

Here is a magnificent illustration of Paul's strange expression, "more than conquerors." Victory is more than victory when the attack is parried, and then answered by a counterthrust that utterly routs the enemy. Victory for the believer is not merely successful resistance to the Devil, but a triumphant offensive against him in the name of the Lord. He is more than conqueror who, in one and the same battle, brings glory to God and shame to the Devil. And temptation takes on an altogether new look when we understand that it provides our Lord Jesus a fresh opportunity to enforce again His victory at the cross, and show His incomparable greatness in us.

Laugh then, in faith, and look to Him, the Lord who leads to victory.

# Chapter Five

Who hath measured the waters in the hollow of his hand, and meted out heaven with the span, and comprehended the dust of the earth in a measure, and weighed the mountains in scales, and the hills in a balance? Who hath directed the Spirit of Jehovah, or being his counsellor hath taught him? With whom took he counsel, and who instructed him, and taught him in the path of justice, and taught him knowledge, and showed to him the way of understanding? Behold, the nations are as a drop of a bucket, and are accounted as the small dust of the balance: behold, he taketh up the isles as a very little thing. And Lebanon is not sufficient to burn, nor the beasts thereof sufficient for a burnt-offering. All the nations are as nothing before him; they are accounted by him as less than nothing and vanity.

To whom then will ye liken God? or what likeness will ye compare unto him? ...

To whom then will ye liken me, that I should be equal to him? saith the Holy One. Lift up your eyes on high, and see who hath created these, that bringeth out their host by number; he calleth them all by name; by the greatness of his might, and for that he is strong in power, not one is lacking....

He giveth power to the faint; and to him that hath no might he increaseth strength. Even the youths shall faint and be weary, and the young men shall utterly fall: but they that wait for Jehovah shall renew their strength; they shall mount up with wings as eagles; they shall run, and not be weary; they shall walk and not faint.

Ho Assyrian, the rod of mine anger, the staff in whose hand is mine indignation. I will send him against a profane nation, and against the people of my wrath will I give him a charge, to take the spoil, and to take the prey, and to tread *them down like the mire of the streets.  Howbeit he meaneth not so, neither doth his heart think so; but it is in his heart to destroy, and to cut off nations not a few.*

*Wherefore it shall come to pass, that, when the Lord hath performed his whole work upon mount Zion and on Jerusalem, I will punish the fruit of the stout heart of the king of Assyria, and the glory of his high looks.  For he hath said, By the strength of my hand I have done it, and by my wisdom; for I have understanding: and I have removed the bounds of the peoples, and have robbed their treasures, and like a Valiant man I have brought down them that sit on thrones: and my hand hath found as a nest the riches of the peoples; and as one gathereth eggs that are forsaken, have I gathered all the earth: and there was none that moved the wing, or that opened the mouth, or chirped.*

*Shall the ax boast itself against him that heweth therewith? shall the saw magnify itself against him that wieldeth it? as if a rod should wield them that lift it up, or as if a staff should lift up him that is not wood.... Look unto me, and be ye saved, all the ends of the earth; for I am God, and there is none else By myself have I sworn, the word is gone forth. from my mouth in righteousness, and shall not return, that unto me every knee shall bow, every tongue shall swear.*
—*Isaiah 40:12-18, 25, 26, 29, 31; 10:5-7, 12-15; 45:22, 23*

# CHRIST, LORD OVER THE NATIONS

So seldom has the threat of war been absent, fear is the normal background to all international relationships. At any period of history, the nations could be divided into those that caused fear, and those that were afraid. The extent of fear in the modern world can be measured by astronomical defense budgets of nations in danger of aggression, and by the equally large budgets of nations thriving on threats. So long have the strong terrified the fearful weak that the promise that "the meek shall inherit the earth" seems a fantasy. Unless he is to be a frustrated escapist, the Christian must be prepared to take a long, cool look at current history. The hermit in his secluded cell, shutting his ears and eyes to the sounds and sights of the world outside, has no scriptural sanction. Isaiah, and all the prophets of Israel, were not afraid to face the terrible reality of a world tormented by threats and fears.

Names change, but conditions remain tragically the same. Assyria, Babylon, Egypt, Syria, Tyre, and other names of ancient times no longer chill our hearts with fear, and some of them have significance only to the historian or archaeologist. But in Isaiah's day, the citizens of Jerusalem felt just as insecure as the people of West Berlin; and Tyre was as terrible in its time as Moscow is in this century. The dangers, tragedies, possibilities and fears were the same; for there is a tragic monotony in the pattern wrought by sin, and war is terrible whether waged with fantastic scientific devices of destruction or fought with the cruel barbaric weapons of olden times. Modern weapons, in fact, kill more swiftly and painlessly than battle-axes and arrows that brought slow and agonizing death. But then, as now, it was not only death that was feared, but the sum total of all the torments of war. Parents prayed that their sons would never be needed to help hold a line of desperate defense; wives pushed to the back of their minds the thought that their husbands might be needed to stand against a slaughtering horde and families tried to forget the threat of famine, wounds, and broken homes that war would inevitably bring.

Human history appears to be a record of the triumph of the wicked, with exceptions so remarkable that a few kings have achieved undying fame merely by being good. The foundation of every great world empire has been laid in blood, and conquered nations have been subjected through fear and suffering. And these processes of the use of force and fear have now reached a dimension that appalls even those who would like to use them. Science that not so long ago was promising us a Utopia now warns that complete destruction is a more likely prospect. Politicians are trying to find the answer to civilization's dilemma by evaluating the relative strength of the opposing nations. The problem is only too clear. Which is stronger, militarily and economically, the Soviet Union or the Western nations? The popular view is that civilization depends on finding the correct answer to that calculation, and because no one in either camp is sure of the solution, threat and counterthreat, fear and greater fear, continue their havoc. But the fear of these days is not different from the fear of Isaiah's time. Suffering may vary in intensity, but death is the same stark terror in all generations, and this is what men ultimately fear, rather than the weapons that cause it.

There is an entirely different point of view. Isaiah saw the Lord God omnipotent reigning, not in theory but in fact; not in the future but now. The hymns that suggest that Jesus our Lord will be crowned at some remote and future date are altogether misleading for "now we see not yet all things subjected to him [i.e., man]. But we behold him who hath been made a little lower than the angels, even Jesus, because of the suffering of death crowned with glory and honor, that by the grace of God he should taste of death for every man" (Heb. 2:8, 9). Isaiah insisted that Christ is Lord over all empires, whether He is acknowledged or not. Final authority does not rest in Washington, Ottawa, London, Paris, or Moscow, but in the hands of our Lord.

Isaiah 40 makes this fact very clear. Handel's magnificent music of "The Messiah" has made us more familiar with the opening words of the chapter than with the great truth it contains. In the middle of the chapter is the remarkable question, "To whom then will ye liken God?" (v. 18), to which the first half (vv. 1-11) gives a well-known answer, and the second half (vv. 12-31) a forgotten reply.

The problem of God's likeness has had a thousand answers. Only a century later than Isaiah, and still six centuries before Christ, the Chinese philosopher Li Pi-yang, known also as Lao-tzu, began his speculations that became the foundations of Taoism. He wrote that "there is something undefined and incomplete, coming into existence before Heaven and Earth. How still it was and formless, standing alone and undergoing no change, reaching everywhere and in no danger of being exhausted. It must be regarded as the Mother of all things. I do not know its name." And in the same book, as he gropes after the ultimate, which he calls The Way, he declares that if he could define it, then it would not be it. In that he was approaching the truth that God cannot be defined, and that all representations of Him are misleading, grotesque, and even blasphemous. Coldly scientific definitions that describe God as First Cause, Force, Mind, or philosophic suggestions that God is Principle or Ideal are, in fact, farther from the truth than Li Pi-yang's simple declaration.

The Bible, however, has an answer for its own profound question. "Behold, the Lord Jehovah will come as a mighty one.... He will feed his flock like a shepherd" (40:10, 11). God is not like any illustrious hero,

85

as idolaters imagine; nor is He like a vague force or idea, as philosophers suggest; but by His own choice He is like a shepherd, and this figure was used throughout Scripture, until the truth shone in supreme clarity when Jesus announced, "I am the good shepherd."

In this chapter (40), Isaiah presents the Shepherd who is promised (vv. 1, 2), prepared for (vv. 3-8), and proclaimed (vv. 9-11). This is Jesus as He is known to the children whose illustrated Bible books depict Him as a bearded, gentle Shepherd, in a long white robe (such as shepherds never wore), holding a crook and carrying a lamb in His arm. This is the Saviour as He is presented constantly in Gospel messages, and rightly so. God is like that in His work of redemption as He seeks for men and women with a concern that we can best understand in terms of a shepherd's patient search for a lost sheep, regardless of what it may cost him. The verbs of verse 1 1 tell us a great deal about the Lord. He "feeds ... gathers ... carries ... and gently leads." The four words list the basic needs of the believer to be gathered into the fellowship of the Church of God, to be spiritually fed, to be guided, and, if need be, to be carried. As a matter of fact, most of us are carried more than we are led, and when we finally reach the heavenly fold it will be because the Lord has done a whole lot of carrying and not because we have followed so well. God is like that. As soon as He sees you falter, He does not abandon you, but picks you up and carries you the rest of the way.

But God is not only like that. Of necessity, in evangelism Christ is pictured as the Shepherd but we have an entirely wrong idea of Him if we think of Him as a meek and humble Man forever associated with Nazareth. A word within the question suggests that a comparison with a shepherd does not tell all the story.

"To whom then will ye liken God?" The inference is that God is incomparable: He is not like anyone. But in verses 12-17 Isaiah seeks a larger scale to measure by, and compares the Lord with the nations.

A suggestion of what is to follow appears in verse 12. The previous verse had spoken of the Lord's arm being for His lambs: this verse speaks of His hand being used to measure the waters. The Lord, therefore, exerts more strength for one young Christian or weak believer than He used in creating the oceans.

The restless, turbulent waters may have suggested to Isaiah's mind the equally restless and apparently uncontrollable nations. What is God like in comparison with the empires that seem to control the destiny of the world, and bring disaster upon the helpless millions? The answer is clear and strong. "Behold, the nations are as a drop of a bucket" (40:15). Do not miss the word behold. The Lord wants us to look intently at the terrible nations before making a comparison with Him. As Isaiah looked beyond his national boundaries to where ruthless armies were poised for attack, and let his imagination dwell upon the horrors of war, he looked up to God and declared with absolute certainty that the nations are just a drop out of a bucket.

When we lived in the city of Luhsien in West China, during World War II, all the water we used was brought by carriers from the Yangtze River to our house. A continuous stream of men rhythmically jogged through the streets between the river and the city, skillfully harmonizing their pace to the beat of the pliant bamboo pole that lifted the weight of the buckets as each step was taken, and allowed the weight to fall when the carrier's leg was straight and the bones in the best position to bear the load. Each bucket was filled to the brim, with a large leaf or flat sticks floating on the surface of the water to prevent spilling. But smoothly as the men moved, it was inevitable that now and then one of the drops that danced on the surface of the water would leap over the side of the bucket. Water cost money in those days, and carrying it was a good living for thousands of coolies, but it was never so precious that a man would stop for the impossible task of trying to recover a lost drop. Neither to him, nor to his thirsty customer, did one drop of water mean anything. The nations are that small before God; they shrink to that insignificance in comparison with our Lord.

But smaller yet, the nations are "accounted as the small dust of the balance" (40:15). I can remember the excitement of experiments, planned and unplanned, as we assembled the apparatus for an afternoon of science in the physics laboratory at high school. A critical part of our paraphernalia was the delicate balance which was kept in a glass case. In spite of that precaution, enough fine dust would sometimes gather on the shining pans to make a perceptible difference in the weights. Those of us who felt that the whole future of the scientific world depended on the accuracy of our measurements usually removed the offending particles by the rather crude method of blowing. Without stopping to consider whether we would add more than we would remove by that method, we gave one hearty blast; and the dust was gone. God can remove any nation just as easily, for they are no more than a particle of dust compared with Him. He blew, and mighty Babylon disappeared in a night. And modern nations, notwithstanding their amazing technological progress, do not constitute any problem for the Lord Jesus, our Good Shepherd, who can overthrow the Soviet Union, or the United States, or any other country as easily as He once dealt with kingdoms of the ancient world.

Nations that fill so many hearts with cold fear are no more than a speck of dust compared with God.

But the comparison has not yet reached its climax. "All the nations are as nothing before him" (40:17). Add together all the resources, good and bad, of all the nations of the world: to the material wealth and military might of the United States add the gigantic resources and formidable power of the USSR and to that add the strength of the British Commonwealth and the countries of the European continent, and to that add the developing resources of India, Pakistan, Formosa, and China, and to the everincreasing total add the products of the revived industries of Japan and other countries of the busy Orient, and to all of this add the manpower of the whole world, and then the grand total in comparison with God is nothing.

"They are accounted by him as less than nothing, and vanity" (40:17). Now the comparison between the Lord and the nations has reached its climax, and we begin to understand the greatness of our incomparable Lord. Jesus, who once spent a few years in the little country of Palestine, is so magnificent a Person that all the nations of our twentieth-century world are a minus quantity in comparison with Him. This is not Isaiah's rhetorical imagery. History is full of proof that the Lord "bringeth princes to nothing" (40:23). Nebuchadnezzar, king of Babylon, is a dramatic example. Strutting on the top of his palace, he looked over the city he had built and boasted, "Is not this the great Babylon which I have built for the royal dwelling-place, by the might of my power and for the glory of my majesty?" But before the question had died upon the king's lips, the unexpected answer came down from Heaven: "O king Nebuchadnezzar, to thee it is spoken: The kingdom is departed from thee: and thou shalt be driven from men;

and thy dwelling shall be with the beasts of the field; thou shalt be made to eat grass as oxen: and seven times shall pass over thee; until thou know that the Most High ruleth in the kingdom of men, and giveth it to whomsoever be will" (Dan. 4: 31, 32). In a split second, the king who had built a city for his royal residence found himself groveling among the beasts, and he who had gone up to the palace roof as a mighty prince came down an insane brute. God spoke, and the king was nothing.

Within recent times, the world has witnessed the same phenomenon without understanding what it saw. Interminable speculation on the death and denunciation of Stalin is ended by the plain truth that God brought him to nothing. Only this can explain the extraordinary enigma of a man, who had elevated himself to the position of a god over his nation, being suddenly repudiated by the nation that had worshiped him. His death, which should have been the final step in his deification by the adoring nation, brought about a downfall so desperate that his very name became anathema. The Lord of the nations brought that miracle about, and He will do it again until the whole world realizes at last what the Church has known all along, that Christ Jesus our Lord and Saviour rules over all nations of the earth and that He does with them whatever He pleases whenever He will. Worldly princes can be made nothing, nations can be reduced to rubble and all the inhabitants of the earth made to realize they are "as grasshoppers" (40:22) before the Lord of all.

This fascinating picture of the greatness of the Lord continues with the original question being asked a second time: "To whom then will ye liken me, that I should be equal to him? saith the Holy One" (40:25). If the shepherd figure is inadequate to the full story of His might, and if the nations are an inadequate measure of

His power, then look to the stars above to seek some standard of greatness there. "See who hath created these, that bringeth out their host by number; he calleth them all by name; by the greatness of his might, and for that he is strong in power, not one is lacking" (40:26).

This chapter is being written in the winter of 1957, which will go down in history as the year when a man-made satellite was hurled into outer space for the first time. When the news broke that Russian scientists had succeeded in sending a few pounds of equipment, enclosed in a small sphere, into an orbit around the earth, the whole world gasped in fearful astonishment. It was an extraordinary achievement but it ought to have increased our amazement at the greatness of our Lord. As telescopes and cameras increase in power, astronomers find it necessary to adjust their estimates of the size of the universe. The constellation named after the beautiful Andromeda has a dim spot of light near her right elbow. This is the most distant object visible to the unaided eye. That blurry speck in the night sky is a nebula of one hundred billion stars whose light takes two million light-years to reach us. No man knows for sure the total number of the stars, but there are at least 100 million galaxies each containing approximately 5 billion stars. This whole intricate system was conceived in the mind of God who, without laboriously making blueprints, or working on a series of experiments, created it and put it into motion; each part moving in its own predetermined orbit and swirling through space at immense speeds; each part integrated with all other parts, forces balancing forces; and all of this done as easily as a man might take a handful of sand to throw across the smooth waters of a silent lake. "By him"—Jesus of Nazareth, the Good Shepherd—"were all things made that are made." If ever you doubt the Good

Shepherd's ability to guide and keep you, look up at the stars and remember that He has kept ,each in its course for billions of centuries, and even now "not one is lacking." If the Lord has never lost one of His stars, He will most certainly not lose track of you. And if ever you know paralyzing fear, look up again, for if He knows the name of every star and sustains it on its course by the "greatness of his might," then He will surely do no less for those who are His children through faith.

But is it possible to be sure that the Lord who is so great does, in fact, take a personal interest in each of us individually? The temptation is to say with Jacob, "My way is hid from Jehovah" (40:27). In spite of modern insistence on the importance of the individual, a person can easily feel lost among the masses and helpless to resist the forces that threaten to destroy us all. And the cynic might easily assert that God, if He exists at all, is more interested in stars than in men. Such views are based on small ideas of the Lord. He is no mere manipulator of stars. "Hast thou not known? hast thou not heard? The everlasting God, Jehovah, the Creator of the ends of the earth, fainteth not, neither is weary; there is no searching of his understanding" (40:28). In answer to the denial that one single person can have the personal attention of God Almighty, the Lord Himself poses a question that is addressed to the doubting individual by its reiterated "thou," and that answers itself. It is as if the Lord takes time out from the enormous responsibility of controlling the universe in order to deal with the urgent matter of a fearful saint who thinks that God is too busy with other matters to notice him.

In His reply, the Lord reveals the qualities which are most needed by the Christian who feels that he has been abandoned by God. In between the first descriptive title of "everlasting God," which declares His self-existence and mighty power, and the third name of "Creator of the ends of the earth," which affirms His general interest in this world, is the name Jehovah which God has chosen for Himself as Saviour. He created the stars; He made the earth; but He is especially concerned with saving men and consequently interested in them individually, since salvation is by personal choice and not by collective decision.

God never faints, either because His strength is exhausted or at the shock of what He sees; and He never becomes weary because of the greatness or difficulty of what He has undertaken. If maintaining the universe from the day that He created it has not exhausted God, then you certainly will not. You can easily and quickly wear out yourself with worry and fear, but you cannot possibly weary Him.

"There is no searching of his understanding," and although it is impossible for us to comprehend an infinite mind or grasp how God can take a personal interest in a million people at the same time, we know it is true for two reasons. If He is able to watch over billions of stars simultaneously, so that not one ever deviates from the course He has prescribed, then the Lord can equally well take care of each of His children. And this is proved in another way by the fact that immediately insignificant Jacob murmured that God did not notice him, the Lord noticed that he had made that remark, and answered him.

As soon as the Lord sees a need, His first concern is to meet it. The words Isaiah uses to describe people in verses 28 and 29 are characteristic of many of God's exhausted saints of the twentieth century. There are those who "faint," those that "have no might," those that are "weary," and those that "utterly fall." If statistics could be obtained, we would probably find that the majority of Christians fall within one or other of those four categories. By the grace of God, those who utterly fall are comparatively few, but the number of the powerless, exhausted and fainthearted is legion. To them all, the Lord offers a share of His unlimited strength. "He giveth power to the faint," and "they that wait for Jehovah shall renew their strength; they shall mount up with wings as eagles; they shall run, and not be weary; they shall walk, and not faint" (40:29, 31).

To walk without fainting is the greatest miracle of all. Most Christians, at some time or other, are able to manage a spectacular flight into the heavenly places, their wings momentarily as strong as an eagle's. At the final day of a great convention, the whole congregation may suddenly take off as they soar to the rare atmosphere of great spiritual heights. Running is also a fairly common phenomenon. At most evangelical churches, the congregation breaks out into a fairly brisk trot regularly every Sunday morning, and follows up with another burst of speed on Wednesday at the prayer meeting. But a steady, consistent walk, up and down hill, fair weather or foul, alone or in company, is rare. It is rare because we do not "wait for Jehovah." A better translation might be "wait upon" or "look to" the Lord. We faint or fall because we do everything except go to the Lord who has an abundance of what we need. Look at the threatening nations, read the news reporters' gloomy prophecies, seek the sorry comfort of the TV, and you soon will faint for fear of the things which are coming on the world. Spend as much time with the Lord as you do with your newspaper and TV, and your strength will be miraculously renewed.

Isaiah 40 is largely concerned with a comparison between God and the nations, but earlier in the prophecy, in chapter 10, is a revelation of how the Lord makes use of the nations to accomplish His will. The exact relationship between godless nations and the Lord Himself is made clear in the words, "Ho Assyrian, the rod of mine anger, the staff in whose hand is mine indignation" (10:5). In a few extraordinary sentences, God reveals that He knew all about the secret war councils of the Assyrian high command. On the one hand, the Lord had determined to chastise His sinning people: "I will send him [the Assyrian] against a profane nation, and against the people of my wrath will I give him a charge, to take the spoil, and to take the prey, and to tread them down like the mire of the streets" (10:6), and on the other hand, the Assyrians had conceived of a war by aggression by which they would "cut off nations not a few" (10:7). Behind those two decisions was the knowledge of the Lord, and the ignorance of the Assyrians. The Assyrians had no inkling of God's intentions or interest in His purposes, but the Lord knew exactly what the Assyrians had planned, and intended to make use of their vicious wars to accomplish what He wanted. The Assyrian "meaneth not so, neither doth his heart think so" (10: 7), and far from having any intention of carrying out God's will, he prepared to lay claim to the title of king of kings by calling his princes kings (10:8). His only motives were love of power and conquest: his methods were destruction and violence. But such a person was admirably fitted for the role of a rod for God to chastise a disobedient nation.

Here is a magnificent revelation of the reality of the Lordship of Christ over the nations. The world appears to be a chaos of secret conferences, malevolent schemes, uncontrolled ambitions, plot and counterplot, propaganda wars, colonial designs, lusting after power, rivalries and suspicion that finally resolve into a precarious balance of smoldering forces. World leaders meet in a search for peace, only to separate in even wider and more dangerous disagreement that drives them back to urgent scheming for their own defense and the downfall of their enemies. Over the chaos is the Lord, manipulating it all to fulfill His will. Fully aware of courses being plotted in the Kremlin, and knowing exactly all decisions being made in the Pentagon, the Lord has devised a master plan in which even sin is made use of to achieve a righteous climax.

The cross of our Lord Jesus Christ is a perfect example of this principle. When we analyze the complex interplay of forces that moved Christ to Calvary, from a human point of view, we find nothing but evil. There were the malevolent designs of Annas and Caiaphas, the cynical injustice of Pilate, the greedy treachery of Judas, the callous mocking by Herod, the brutal cruelty of the Roman soldiery, the cynical complacency of the Sanhedrin, and the blood-thirsty clamor of the rabble, but the outcome of all those evils was the will of God. Each man, according to his own free choice, played to the full his evil part in the mighty drama, but when Jesus finally hung upon the cross, limp and dying, it was only and entirely by the will of God who sent the Son to be the Saviour of the world. When sin had done its utmost, the outcome was the remedy for sin.

The rule of the Lord over the nations, therefore, is real and practical. It is a miracle on a vast scale. Seldom openly interfering with the course of human history, and apparently allowing men full liberty to pursue their individual evil ways, God so manipulates these terrible forces, which to us often appear uncontrolled and uncontrollable, that the final result is exactly what

He purposed from the beginning. The church of the first century was able to face fierce persecution and incredible odds because they constantly rejoiced in this magnificent truth. When fires of persecution first began to blaze after the miraculous healing of the lame beggar in the temple, the church met to consider the threatening attitude of the Jewish high council that had already condemned their Lord to death, and Peter and John to silence. In prayer, those believers recalled the violent opposition to their Saviour against whom "both Herod and Pontius Pilate, with the Gentiles and the peoples of Israel, were gathered together, to do whatsoever thy hand and thy counsel foreordained to come to pass" (Acts 4:27, 28). Pilate and Herod doing God's will; the whole evil world doing God's will: doing it in ignorance but nevertheless doing exactly what God had predetermined before the world began.

The ignorant fulfillment of God's will by a sinful nation or individual has no merit. Assyria, who had no intention of carrying out the divine purpose, was not made virtuous by becoming the rod of God's anger. The strap, now so seldom used, does not become noble by being used on a delinquent schoolboy, now so often found. As to doing God's will, Assyria "meaneth not so, neither doth his heart think so; but it is in his heart to destroy, and to cut off nations not a few" (10:7). Assyria, therefore, was not chosen because of its righteousness, and was not made righteous by being chosen of God. This fact disproves the common argument that victory in war can be predicted on the basis of relative righteousness. In the last two terrible conflicts that have swept over the world, the Western nations have optimistically encouraged themselves to believe that they would finally win the day because they were more righteous than their enemies. In World War 1, England felt herself to be more righteous than a foe she regarded as the ungodly Hun. The atheistic French probably had the same views in those days; and German Christians, hearing atrocity stories that were not always propaganda, undoubtedly believed that victory should, and would, be to the righteous.

In our day, not a few find comfort in thinking that godless Russia could not be successful against God-fearing America. The argument would be true of a nation that wholeheartedly recognized the Lordship of Jesus Christ, and faithfully obeyed Him so that politics, society, education and every other part of national life was in full accord with God's revealed will. But for a nation that has known the truth and deliberately turned away from it, the other principle is far more relevant that God will use a heathen nation as the instrument of His wrath against an apostate people. Israel was sent against the Amalekites, not because of the righteousness of Israel, but because of the sin of Amalek; Assyria was sent against Israel, not because of Assyrian righteousness but because of Israel's departure from the Lord they had once known. Victory was given to a godless nation against a sinning people of God.

The so-called Christian nations of this century, therefore, have no reason for smug complacency in their own security because of the wickedness of their enemies. The godliness of our forefathers, or the presence of a godly remnant among us, is no more a guarantee that God will not use Russia, or any other pagan nation, as the rod of His anger against us, than the presence of Isaiah and other godly men insured Israel's deliverance from the Assyrian hordes. Russia is no worse than Assyria: and the western nations are no better than Israel.

The Assyrian, flushed with victory, boasted of his

triumphs in words that are amazingly modern. "By the strength of my hand I have done it, and by my wisdom; for I have understanding: and I have removed the bounds of the peoples, and have robbed their treasures, and like a valiant man I have brought down them that sit on thrones: and my hand hath found as a nest the riches of the peoples; and as one gathereth eggs that are forsaken, have I gathered all the earth: and there was none that moved the wing, or that opened the mouth, or chirped" (10:13, 14). Apart from a few minor alterations to modernize the verbs, these words are a ready-made speech for any national leader, sounding off on a day of victory. "Victory has come to our nation this day," he says, "because of our superior resources, and because we have the know-how. We have redrawn the map of the world, exhausted the enemy, brought down to the dust this tyrant that brought so much misery on us all, and now our foes lie silent and disarmed before us." Assyrian rhetoric seems to have set the pattern for all time, and deluded men into thinking that victory is always the result of greater material strength and national ingenuity. Assuming that the enemy, actual or probable, is more wicked than we are, and that we are stronger than he is, we count on victory. The Bible offers no encouragement for that kind of thinking, but on the contrary mocks it. "Shall the ax boast itself against him that heweth therewith? shall the saw magnify itself against him that wieldeth it? as if a rod should wield them that lift it up" (10:15). Assyria never gained victory: God gave it them. They had nothing to boast of; the Lord had used them to carry out His predetermined purpose as a woodsman might take his ax to cut down a tree already marked for felling because of its rottenness. The Lord has never been subject to the will of any nation, either in peace or war.

The danger of failing to realize this truth is extremely grave. Assyria perished for no other reason. The first word of verse 16 tells the story. "Therefore" (10:16); because they boasted of a victory which was not theirs, but which was granted to them as the rod of God's anger, "the Lord, Jehovah of hosts, will send among his fat ones leanness; and under his glory there shall be kindled a burning like the burning of fire" (10: 16). When they dared to rob God of His glory, the Assyrians signed their own death warrant. Having carried out His purpose, the Lord destroyed the nation as quickly and easily as a man might throw away a blunted ax-head and burn the handle in the fire. Assyria's collapse was to be so swift that Isaiah compares it with a forest fire so devastating that the surviving trees could be counted by a child (10: 19). The Assyrian Empire was no more significant than a drop in the bucket, or a speck of dust on a pan, or nothing and less than nothing. God blew, and they were not. And the mute testimony of ruined and buried cities that archaeologists can discover only with difficulty is confirmation that the Lord did not speak in vain.

That Christ is Lord over the nations, and does with them as He pleases, is a secret known only to His people. God has revealed the mystery to us that current events might not disturb our peace of heart and mind, or divert our attention from the triumphant climax of His plan. In these fantastic days in which we live, Christians will find reassurance in the Bible, and ought to read with amused skepticism the pitiful predictions of newspaper writers. God makes the news: man can only record it. Every believer has the privilege of entering into a quiet rest that comes from knowing that Jesus is Lord. "O my people that dwellest in Zion," says your Lord, "be not afraid of the Assyrian, though he smite thee with the rod, and lift up his staff against thee, after the manner of Egypt. For yet a very little while, and the indignation against thee shall be accomplished, and mine anger shall be directed to his destruction" (10:24, 25). Only an unshakable conviction that Christ is mightier than all nations, and has them fully under His control, can deliver us from fear and give us peace, even if the prospect remains of war "for yet a very little while." Our views of prophecy cannot change facts, and we cannot expect God to adjust His plans to fit in with our prophetic charts, but our view of Christ will certainly determine how we face the events of today, and the more terrible events that tomorrow will bring. The great fact of the future, that already casts its light upon us like a brilliant star climbing steadily into the night sky, is the appearing of our Lord and Saviour after the present little while has passed.

Christ's recognition as Lord is now limited to the minority who know Him as Saviour. The world would either ridicule the idea that all things are under His feet, or blame Him for the chaos we are in, forgetting that our calamities are not due to His inefficiency, but to man's refusal to submit to Him. We cannot blame either the law or the police for the existence of crime: the cause is the rejection of the law on the part of some who want to do just as they please. God would not be satisfied that this state of affairs should continue indefinitely, or that the rule of His Son over the nations should be indirect and involuntary. He has sworn that this shall be changed.

The Bible contains at least four mighty oaths of God; two of them are in the Epistle to the Hebrews, and two are in Isaiah. In Hebrews 3: 1 1, part of Psalm 95 is quoted to prove that the unbeliever shall never know rest. "As I swear in my wrath, They shall not enter into my rest. Take heed, brethren, lest haply there shall be in any one of you an evil heart of unbelief, in falling away from the living God." The unbeliever, whose life is characterized by a fidgety and frustrated restlessness now, is condemned to that state perpetually. In Hebrews 6:17, God swears that the believer shall most assuredly obtain all that God has promised. Our hopes of eternal blessing are anchored in the unchangeable facts that God cannot lie, cannot fail, cannot change, and that our Forerunner has already reached the place of blessing ahead of us. The third oath is in Isaiah 14:24 where God swears that His enemy the Assyrian shall be broken, and the deduction seems valid that God will deal with all His enemies in the same way. And the fourth oath declares: "By myself have I sworn, the word is gone forth from my mouth in righteousness, and shall not return, that unto me every knee shall bow, every tongue shall swear" (45:23). These are the four great pillars of certainty upon which the future rests. The unbeliever shall be eternally restless; the believer shall be eternally blessed; all opposition to God shall cease; and Christ shall be universally acknowledged as Lord.

God has sworn this with an oath that is not for the purpose of dispelling His own doubts, but for convincing others who may be in doubt. Men use oaths to impress, or to bide their lies; God uses oaths that His people might know that the truths He speaks are as unchangeable as Himself. Neither Russia nor the United States will finally dominate the world, but Christ our Lord, who will be openly accepted as sovereign King by every living man and woman in every continent, country, and island. In the steamy jungles of Burma, across the wide prairies, in the great capitals, on remote Pacific islands, in distant mountain kingdoms; in countries now communistic and in countries that are free; and in New

102

York, Berlin, Baghdad, Harbin, Calcutta, Leopoldville, and wherever men are found, Jesus will be accepted as Lord. Travelers will never cross the frontiers of His kingdom for it will extend everywhere; airplanes will never fly over territory that is not His, for all lands will be His; and radio will never beam its messages to hostile nations, for all peoples will be subject to Him.

This mighty oath has gone out of God's mouth "in righteousness" (45:23) which is a declaration that righteousness demands that Jesus should reign. We began this chapter by saying that history seems to record the triumph of the wicked. We close the chapter by emphasizing that God has sworn that evil cannot finally prevail. Sinners certainly have a temporary success. In their small way, individual sinners deceive themselves into thinking that they can sin and get away with it. In a larger way, infamous men have built empires on ruthlessness and unrestrained evil. Men have been under the delusion that God can be defied with impunity. Karl Marx taught that religion, and especially the Christian religion, with its exhortations to suffer meekly the inequalities, injustices, and trials of this life in the hope of a future happiness in the world to come, was one of the major causes of evil, and ought therefore to be removed. The spectacular success of Communism, that began with a vicious attack upon religion and upon God Himself, has increased their confidence that man shall rule the world, and that if God exists He is of very little importance.

By winning half the world for their cause, communists have achieved in less than fifty years something that the Church has never accomplished in nearly two thousand years of evangelism, and on a statistical basis they have every reason to be sure that world dominion is slowly but inevitably coming within their grasp. Former world conquerors were just as confident. Success in battle or conquest through fear seemed to guarantee a world empire beneath their godless feet, but they never knew that at the height of their spectacular victories they were nothing more than an ax in the hand of God, or the rod of His anger. Much less did they understand that God has ordained a day when Jesus shall emerge from His chosen obscurity to dazzle the world with His glorious reign of righteousness.

The last that the world saw of Christ was His lifeless body banging limp from a criminal's cross. Justice and truth, righteousness and honor were trampled in the dust that day, and sin shouted for joy that the King of righteousness was dead. The world has never reversed its decision or changed its opinion of that dark deed, and God apparently has done little about it. But He will reverse that unrighteous decision on the day when His oath is made good that every knee shall bow to His once-rejected Son.

All who have accepted Christ as Saviour and Lord have already knelt before Him. We were not dazzled by the brightness of His appearance, but moved by the glory of His grace. We were not forced reluctantly to our knees by His terrible appearance as Judge and Ruler of the nations, but we knelt before Him at His cross, knowing no compulsion but the constraint of His redemptive love. His bleeding head and hands and feet brought us to our knees, and of our own free will we gave ourselves to Him, offering up sword and shield, that we might become knights of the Most High.

That is conversion. It is more than the easy gesture of raising a hand in an evangelistic campaign: it is more than going forward at the altar call. It is going down on your knees to acknowledge that Jesus Christ is to be forever your only Lord and Master, whose will is never

to be contested or resisted.  It is an absolute surrender
to an absolute Lord.

# Chapter Six

And there shall come forth a shoot out of the stock of Jesse, and a branch out of his roots shall bear fruit. And the Spirit of Jehovah shall rest upon him, the spirit of wisdom and understanding, the spirit of counsel and might, the spirit of knowledge and of the fear of Jehovah. And his delight shall be in the fear of Jehovah; and he shall not judge after the sight of his eyes, neither decide after the hearing of his ears; but with righteousness shall he judge the poor, and decide with equity for the meek of the earth; and he shall smite the earth with the rod of his mouth; and with the breath of his lips shall he slay the wicked. And righteousness shall be the girdle of his waist, and faithfulness the girdle of his loins.

And the wolf shall dwell with the lamb, and the leopard shall lie down with the kid; and the calf and the young lion and the fatling together; and a little child shall lead them. And the cow and the bear shall feed; their young ones shall lie down together; and the lion shall eat straw like the ox. And the suckling child shall play on the hole of the asp, and the weaned child shall put his hand on the adder's den. They shall not hurt nor destroy in all my holy mountain; for the earth shall be full of the knowledge of Jehovah, as the waters cover the sea.

And it shall come to pass in that day, that the root of Jesse, that standeth for an ensign of the peoples, unto him shall the nations seek; and his resting-place shall be glorious.

—Isaiah 11: 1-10

# CHRIST THE LORD
# OF ALL CREATION

THE TITLE OF LORD, as applied to Christ, is unqualified. He is not Lord of this, but not of that. He is Lord of all, without exception. The Greeks used the word for men of authority, and centuries later in feudal England the word became a title of honor conferred by the king on heads of the great families that divided the country between them and ruled in the sovereign's name. The titles have survived to modern times although much of the ancient authority and former privileges have long ago disappeared. In parts of England there is still a lord of the manor whose title dates back to the times when land held by a lord was divided among freehold tenants over whom he held authority. London still has its lord mayor, and the chief administrator of law is still called the lord chief justice. And in the house of Lords, the illustrious heads of noble families that shaped the course of English history retain a fading glory as they debate great matters of state. Outside of their manors, cities, or country, none of these men have any authority at all. Should any one of them direct his dignified steps toward North America, he would more probably be offered a part in Hollywood than a castle.

In saying that Jesus is Lord, we make no limitations. He rules over every creature and everything everywhere. He is Lord in Heaven; He is Lord over all worlds. He is Lord of the angels, and Lord over Satan and all the powers of darkness. He is Lord of His Church, and Lord over all the nations. He is Lord over all things, animate and inanimate.

The degree in which Christ is recognized as Lord

varies very much. The angels accept Him without question as their sovereign Lord, and instantly obey Him. The Church is as quick to call Him Lord as she is slow to do His will. Satan and his legions cannot deny that Christ is Lord, but resolutely resist Him. For this reason, the Lordship of Christ is being enforced in successive stages. In Isaiah 11 we find a revelation of conditions on the earth when Christ shall be the uncontested Ruler who will redeem all that fell under the curse.

When a Roman soldier twisted a bunch of thorns into a wreath to press upon the head of Christ, he cannot have known that every thorn is a result of sin. A terrible change swept over nature on the day when Adam listened to his wife rather than to God. "Because thou hast hearkened unto the voice of thy wife," said God, "and hast eaten of the tree, of which I commanded thee, saying, Thou shalt not eat of it: cursed is the ground for thy sake; in toil shalt thou eat of it all the days of thy life; thorns also and thistles shall it bring forth to thee; and thou shalt eat the herb of the field; in the sweat of thy face shalt thou eat bread." By bitter experiment Adam learned that enlightenment promised by the Devil is the greatest of all deceptions, and that sin leads only to hardship, difficulty, and darkness. The abnormality of thorns and thistles set the stage for the long struggle between man and nature. The curse upon the earth has that rare and delicate balance between grace and judgment that characterizes all God's dealings with man. Thorns and thistles were a judgment that constantly handicap progress, but grace insured that man could survive by the sweat of his brow. Thorns, as centuries later Paul was to discover, would not be removed lest ease of life might lead men to a proud independence of God, but grace would always be sufficient.

And to this day, the soil that so liberally supplies luxuriant crops of weeds but so reluctantly yields harvest of useful plants, is a stubborn witness to the fact that man has sinned.

The sin of man has likewise affected all the animals. Because it had beguiled Eve, God said to the serpent: "Because thou hast done this, cursed art thou above all cattle" (Gen. 3:14). At that time the serpent was "more subtle than any beast of the field which Jehovah God had made," which suggests that it exceeded all other animals in intelligence. For this reason, and because Satan would be most unlikely to choose any lesser animal, the serpent was probably king of the beasts. Mythology offers evidence to confirm this. The Chinese, whose continuous history is among the longest in the world, have a high place in their myths for the great five-clawed winged dragon and embroidered its likeness on the silk robes of their emperors. This association of the dragon with royal power cannot have been accidental, but suggests that the mythical dragon is identical with the serpent in its original form as assumed by Satan.

Because of its cooperation in the Devil's purpose, the king of the beasts and his kingdom came under a curse. The serpent was cursed "above all cattle," and other animals, therefore, must have suffered in some way, but less severely than their king whose form was so changed that he was thenceforth compelled to grovel in the dust. The record of Eve's temptation by the serpent suggests that the animals originally had power of speech or some easy way of communicating with man. Had it been otherwise, Eve would have been so astonished or terrified at hearing a serpent talk that she would have immediately rushed off to find Adam without waiting to hear what the animal had to say. She most certainly would not have continued the conversation as if it were quite commonplace for a woman and a snake to talk together. Probably, then, in Eden the animals could speak, and the story of Balaam riding to curse Israel (Num. 22) confirms this. On that occasion, the Lord "opened the mouth of the ass" so that it spoke to rebuke its master. The curse reduced the vocabulary of the animals to incoherent chatterings, squeaks, growls, snarls, and roars. Only the loquacious parrot, and a few of his feathered friends, retain any trace of its former powers.

By the curse, the animals lost their purpose. God surely never created a hippopotamus only to fill a large tank in a zoo, or a lion merely to be an entertainer in a circus. The problem becomes greater when we try to guess the reason for the existence of the malaria-carrying mosquito, or the disease-distributing fly. Horse and cow, cat and dog, sheep and goat, and all the domestic animals have an important function in the life of man, but to what purpose is the skunk or the hyena, the giraffe or the kangaroo, and lice or fleas? The need for food and clothing has forced men to eat the flesh and use the skin of most animals, but reason rebels at the idea that God designed a snake merely to provide soft skin for a woman's shoes or handbag, and created the kangaroo only to give the biologists an interesting subject to study.

The animal world may have lost its power of speech, and it appears to be lacking in purpose. It certainly has been subjected to fear. The discords of man's life have their echoes in the animal kingdom. Soon after man first sinned, death began to stalk in the jungles, and fear to lurk in all the shadows. Dog chases cat, and cat chases the elusive rat. The lion preys upon the harmless deer, until he himself falls to the hunter's gun. How did all this fear and strife begin? Why did a wolf first slink away at the sight of a man? And why does a bird, even now, fly away from the curious, but harmless, bird-watcher—armed with nothing more terrible than a camera? Animal fear began right after the Flood. When Noah came out of the ark, God promised him: "And the fear of thou and the dread of you shall be upon every beast of the earth, and upon every bird of the heavens; with all wherewith the ground teemeth, and all the fishes of the sea, into your band are they delivered" (Gen. 9:2). At that time, Noah and his family were greatly outnumbered by the animals who, after being shut up for a year without room to exercise or fresh food to eat, were so ravenously hungry and ready for the chase that they might easily have forgotten how much they were indebted to the captain of their ship and swallowed him whole.

The truth, however, lies deeper. Man's moral fitness to rule was lost when he sinned. Ruling in God's name is dependent upon being like Him. The emergency measures God put into operation when the four men and their wives came out of the ark included the device of fear to keep the animals in their proper places and prevent them from rising against their fallen masters to destroy what little remained of the human race.

To those who complain that "nature in the raw is seldom mild," the Bible answers that God did not so create it. Nature became that way through man's revolt against God's authority. The root of the trouble is not in Nature, but in man who was made "to have dominion over the works of thy hands." The psalm continues with the declaration: "Thou hast put all things under his feet: all sheep and oxen, yea, and the beasts of the field, the birds of the heavens, and the fish of the sea, whatsoever passeth through the paths of the seas"

(Ps. 8:6-8). Man's failure left the animal world without its rightful lord.

This, then, is the chaotic condition of the world with which our Lord Jesus intends to deal. In Isaiah 11 we are told how that day will be ushered in, and what it will be like.

Reclamation begins with a miracle. From a dried up, lifeless stump emerges a tender shoot that is to restore all Nature to its pristine glory. "And there shall come forth a shoot out of the stock of Jesse, and a branch out of his roots shall bear fruit" (11:1). The Saviour of mankind appears to come forth from a race, spiritually sterile and under the curse. Isaiah must have puzzled over this mystery he had uttered by inspiration, and tried to reconcile what be knew of the stock of Jesse with the unique character and astonishing program of the mysterious Branch which was to grow out of that family. Centuries later, Zechariah spurred on the flagging zeal of the builders of Jerusalem with the promise from the Lord: "I will bring forth my servant the Branch" (netzer), but Matthew it was who finally identified Him as Jesus a Nazarene. "Existing in the form of God" He was "found in fashion as a man."

Verses 2 and 3 describe His enduement with power; verses 4 and 5 disclose the principle by which He works; and verses 6 through 16 describe the program.

"And the Spirit of Jehovah shall rest upon him, the spirit of wisdom and understanding" (v. 2). That describes the intellectual life of the Lord Jesus. Psychologists define intelligence as the ability to solve intellectual problems on the basis of past experience, and a grasp of the essentials. Or, more shortly, intelligence is intellect put to use. Jesus will do exactly that. On the basis of His infinite knowledge of creation, extending back to the time when He Himself made all things, and understanding perfectly the problem of sin and its devastation, which He has watched since its beginning, He will restore order to this chaotic world. He has begun already in individual hearts and lives by unfailingly solving every tangled problem and impossible difficulty submitted to Him in faith.

The Lord Jesus has also the "spirit of counsel and might" which refer to His practical ability. "Counsel" is the ability to come to a right conclusion, and "might" is the power to carry out the decision with energy. Never forget that Christ is a Man of action. His life upon earth was a tremendous demonstration of the energy with which He successfully deals with every kind of practical problem. His analysis of the difficulty, and diagnosis of the root causes were swift and accurate: and the remedy was immediately applied whenever His diagnosis was accepted, and his help asked. Whenever the trouble was honestly and completely committed to Him, He never had the slightest difficulty in solving it because His power is unlimited. New men and women were the result.

A few years ago, one Sunday morning, I stood outside a fairly large church in northern Japan, watching the Christians arriving for the service. After living in the Orient for several years, I scarcely noticed the colorful kimonos of the women, the uniforms of the students, or the wooden shoes that had once so attracted my attention, but I immediately noticed the unusual sight of a whole family arriving at the church. In a land where so many churches have congregations composed almost entirely of young people whose parents are not Christians, or of individual believers from families otherwise entirely Buddhist or Shinto, a Christian family is so rare that there is no expression in Japanese for Christian home. When I asked a Japanese church

113

worker about the family, she smiled and told me a typically complicated story that involved a faithless husband, an unscrupulous woman, a despairing wife, and threats of murder, divorce, and suicide. The account was so long and intricate that I could not keep all the details straight, and if the whole story were to be told a medium-sized novel would be the result. The case was a counselor's nightmare. "But," said the woman who told me the story, "we told the Lord all about it. It took us seven years of hard praying. First the wife was converted; then the other members of the family, one by one; and now they are all saved, and regularly give each month almost the entire amount of my support for the work of the Lord." The counsel and might of Christ had worked another miracle in Japan.

If reading this has brought to your mind some stubborn problem for which the solution has long remained elusive, bring the matter to the Lord Jesus. He can solve it.

Third, He has the "spirit of knowledge and of the fear of Jehovah." This describes His spiritual life in which knowledge was founded on the fellowship of love, and fear was expressed as reverence. The Bible nowhere teaches that the believer should be terrified of God as men might cringe before a cruel tyrant, but there is a proper understanding of the indescribable majesty and holiness of God that issues in a wholesome fear lest we should tamper with His glory, or trespass upon His prerogatives. In His earthly life, Christ perfectly demonstrated this attitude which is described in the beautiful words, "the fear of Jehovah is fragrance to him" (11:3, marg.).

Many of the old churches of Europe were built as if the architect, craftsmen, congregation, and minister had all agreed that the house of God should be no ordinary place, but should impress upon all who entered its doors the need for reverence in the presence of the Lord. The design of the buildings was to that one end. The gray stone walls and sloping roof were dwarfed either by a tower whose bells pealed chimes of praise, or by a spire whose thin finger pointed upward to the heavens. The deep colors of the stained-glass windows robbed the daylight of its glare and created rainbow hues that chased the dark shadows from the tall columns supporting the vaulted roof. Old oaken pulpits, somehow giving the impression that they had never been occupied by any except solemn men, robed and dignified, speaking forth in sonorous tones the Word of God, looked down upon the silent rows of pews where even a smile would seem out of place. And the lectern with its purple velvet covering and faded golded tassels, carried an open Bible ready for any who cared to push open the heavy wooden doors beneath the carved archway of the church entrance. Even profane visitors, who are interested only in antiquities or the burial places of their European ancestors or favorite poet, find themselves walking softly and talking in whispers as they move slowly down the aisle that countless worshipers of another generation have trod.

Ritual may have robbed many churches of their power, and ancient forms may have hidden the truths of the Gospel, but that can never justify abandoning a wholesome fear of God and reverence in His Presence. The method of approach to God has changed since the days when once a year a trembling high priest stood within the Most Holy Place of the tabernacle, before the mysterious glory that covered the mercy seat; but God has not changed, and boldness in approaching the throne of grace is no excuse for a casual familiarity with God. Those who regard candles, stained glass, priestly robes, and every kind of ecclesiastical furniture as diluted popery have sometimes confused ritual with reverence, and in rejecting the first have forgotten the second, until their churches have become centers where morning worship begins with whispered gossip that gradually merges into noisy exuberance as they praise the Lord without ever becoming awed at the remembrance that "he is thy Lord; and reverence thou him." This is not an argument for ritual but a call for reverence in a day when many evangelical Christians have forgotten, or never known, that the fear of the Lord was fragrant to our Saviour.

The principle by which Christ will carry out His program of restoration is righteousness (11: 4, 5): "With righteousness shall he judge the poor. . . . And righteousness shall be the girdle of his waist." The Spirit of the Lord would rest upon Him, not for spectacular displays or sensational exhibitions, but for the enforcement of righteousness. Departure from righteousness was the root cause of the ruin of the world; and a return to righteousness is the method of restoration. When the world is to be put right, then it will first be made right with God, and as soon as this principle begins to operate, a social revolution takes place. The triumphant wicked disappear to make place for a group that has never yet rated very highly. "With righteousness shall he judge the poor, and decide for equity for the meek of the earth; and he shall smite the earth with the rod of his mouth; and with the breath of his lips shall he slay the wicked" (I 1:4). The same righteousness that demands that Christ shall have His rightful place of honor insists that the meek shall at last inherit the earth, and the wicked perish in the grave. A novelist in search of inspiration might well consider writing a story of a sinless world. The difficulty would-be that the imagi-

116

nation would be strained to the utmost in describing a society without thieves, adulterers, liars, and murderers. Sin is a big business in the modern world, and radio, TV, newspapers, and novels depend on crime, or the possibility of wrongdoing, for their news or themes. But when Christ asserts His lordship over this earth we shall witness the astonishing sight of the whole of civilization based on righteousness.

The program of restoration extends to the animal kingdom (1 1: 6-9). Luther, Calvin, Vitringa, and others interpret these verses symbolically because of the difficulty of accepting them literally. A rapidly decreasing company of theological optimists see here a beautiful allegory of a brave new world in which even the bad people finally come around to seeing that the good people are after all quite nice, and accepting a better way of life, they slap each other on the back with cries of "Brother!", and live happily ever after. But even those who once dreamed of a man-made millennium now hesitate to predict that the Golden Age is just around the atomic corner.

Understanding of Scripture is dependent on knowledge of God. If we accept the fact that with Him all things are possible, then no difficulty remains in accepting these verses as a description of what will literally take place when Jesus reigns on the earth. All nature will be in harmony; the animals will have a new nature; and man will have his lost authority restored.

The distinction between domestic and wild animals and the perpetual hostility between pairs of animals will at last come to an end when wolf and lamb, leopard and kid, calf and lion cub are all subject to the rule of Christ. A harmony that only Adam and Eve have witnessed will then be universal. This harmony among the animals, as among men, will be the consequence of a new nature. The cow and the bear shall feed together, and the lion shall eat straw like an ox (11:7). At the present time it is physically impossible for a lion to eat like an ox because its mouth is constructed for tearing flesh and crunching bones, and not for ruminating like an ox. Only by a miracle could a lion eat like an ox, but God who created the lion can certainly make the small adjustment necessary to alter its feeding methods. If God can give man a new nature, He can certainly give a lion a different mouth.

Man's restored authority over the animal kingdom is promised in fascinating terms that are reminiscent of the very beginning of human history. "A little child shall lead them" (11:6), and "the sucking child shall play on the hole of the asp, and the weaned child shall put his hand on the adder's den" (11:8). A tiny baby in those wonderful days yet to come will play unafraid beside the hole of the very animal through which sin entered the world; for the snake will have lost its venom, and little children will learn leadership and responsibility by exercising over the animals the authority first given to Adam.

Throughout the Scripture record the animals give more obedience to God than do men. In Noah's day every animal given the opportunity entered the ark, but of the people invited only Noah's immediate family responded. Men are dumb, not the animals. When the Philistines made a test to find out whether their calamities were due to the capture of the ark of God or not, two cows carried the ark back to Israel in obedience to the Lord's command. The ravens that regularly brought food to Elijah twice a day were God's faithful servants, and the great fish that swallowed Jonah was in exactly the right place at precisely the right moment. Balaam's ass was more obedient to the Lord than his master, and the hungry lions were all subject to God's will when they shut their mouths in spite of the temptation of Daniel's presence. A fish obediently delivered the tax money for Christ and Peter just when it was needed, and the unbroken colt that carried the Saviour into Jerusalem was perfectly responsive to the gentle guiding of His hand in spite of the shouts and waving palms. We cannot even guess how God conveyed His will to these animals, or know if they consciously obeyed Him. They certainly played an important part in fulfilling His purposes, and the record of their obedience gives us a hint of what the earth will be like when it is "full of the knowledge of Jehovah, as the waters cover the sea" (11:9). The animals then will surely find their purpose in a world wholly subject to the Lord Jesus.

In that great day when all things shall be restored to their former glory, all the nations shall seek Christ (11:10). That is, for the first time in the history of the world, nations will turn to Christ instead of away from Him. Statesmen will no longer seek for formulas, but for the will of Christ; foreign secretaries will no more scurry to New York, London, or Paris to settle their differences or map out their strategy, but go to Jerusalem to receive their instructions from the Lord of all the earth. Enmities as ancient as the bitter rivalry between Judah and Israel will die at last; for the smoldering fire of envy will be forever extinguished when the Lord not only brings war to an end but removes its basic causes (11:13).

Even geography will be changed to harmonize with the new conditions. The river Euphrates will be divided into seven streams, and part of the Red Sea will be dried up. If anyone objects to taking this prophecy literally, then you do not know God. When He sets out to make over this old world, He will do a perfect job, and the adjustment of rivers and mountains will be a minor matter for One so great as He. It ought to be obvious that the world needs some geographical adjustment. If popular opinion is at all right, then an ideal climate hardly exists anywhere in the world, and badly needs improvement. The great parched deserts of northern Africa and central Asia, and vast areas of the icy polar regions, as well as the dense forests, refuse to yield their untold acres to useful purpose.

The purposelessness of Nature is its greatest mystery. Beyond and around this world are at least 100 million galaxies each containing 5 billion stars. Within each atom is a little universe of electrons, protons, and neutrons moving in their orbits. On the earth and in the earth, in the sea and in the air, life teems in every form and shape. In the murky depths of the ocean, fish swim in perpetual darkness. When Capt. Jacques-Yves Cousteau recently took his ship "Calypso" over the Romanche Trench in the Atlantic, a specially designed underwater camera took photographs at 24,600 feet below sea level and showed that life exists in those dark depths where the pressure is so tremendous that the 1½" plate glass of the lens guard was cracked. The miracle of life under such conditions is matched by the mystery of its purpose.

What Isaiah saw dimly was revealed to Paul clearly. For years I read Romans 8 without the faintest idea of what the middle section of that magnificent chapter is about. The use of the word creature (v. 19) in the King James Version is altogether misleading. J. B. Phillips' stimulating translation removes the obscurity. "The whole creation is on tiptoe to see the wonderful sight of the sons of God coming into their own." It is not a creature that impatiently awaits deliverance, but the whole of creation.

This generation, more than any other, is realizing

the awful possibilities of Nature's secrets being discovered by wicked men. The first use made of knowledge of forces that hold the atom together was the obliteration of the cities of Hiroshima and Nagasaki. If men had been able to unravel these mysteries easily or earlier, there is no doubt that civilization would long ago have perished by the hand of some ruthless Lamech or his kin. God subjected creation to futility, locking away its secrets, lest man should destroy himself. In spite of all its latent powers, waiting to unfold in all their glory like the petals of a rose in June, Nature has been condemned to wait. But not for the cold and lifeless fate which scientists predict for the universe. "It has been given hope" (Rom. 8:20). Now, like Sleeping Beauty, all. Nature awaits the coming of her Prince. And come He will to rescue the whole of created life from the "tyranny of change and decay" (Rom. 8:21).

The Lord will bring about the transformation of Nature through the band of redeemed men. The whole creation of God "coming into their own"! The cycle will then be complete. Through Adam's disobedience, he lost his power to rule the world in God's name, and he was left to ponder the riddle of the universe. Only God has the full answer which He will reveal to those who are His sons, not only by creation but by the new birth. The first test of obedience was a tree. Adam ate its forbidden fruit and died. The second test of obedience is likewise a tree on which the Saviour hung and died.

God's work of the redemption of all things, therefore, begins at the very point where all things came under the curse. It begins with man. Whenever a man agrees with God's verdict that he is a sinner, and prays for forgiveness and cleansing through the death of Christ upon the cross, that man is redeemed from the

121

guilt and curse of sin, and made a son of God. That is the essence of the Gospel, but it is not all. The redemptive process that begins in the human heart will continue until all is reclaimed. Not only those who receive Christ as Saviour, but every tree and plant, bird and beast, star and planet, fish and fowl is to be liberated from the ancient curse, and its purpose revealed. Nature will have "magnificent liberty" and find its purpose in magnifying the Lord. And then every gently opening bud will declare His fragrance, every full-throated bird will sing His praise, every creeping thing fulfill His will, and all the universe will be filled with the starry symphony of a new and greater Hallelujah chorus. And men and women who have been made new creatures by the second birth will see all around fresh evidence that Christ is Lord to the glory of God the Father.

If creation waits with impatient eagerness for the day of liberation, much more the believer in Christ. We experience in a smaller way the frustration felt by Nature on its vast scale. Remember that when you are tempted to judge another Christian. If his imperfect personality bothers you, it may bother him even more; and if you feel that he ought to be very different from what he is, he himself may be longing for the day when he will be rid of the handicap of an unredeemed body and imperfect mind. The physical body is not changed by conversion; it comes under the new management of the Holy Spirit, but it does not become a new body. It remains part of unredeemed creation, and does not therefore readily cooperate in spiritual activities. The believer, for example, seldom gets active help from his body when he decides to pray. His body will show a marked preference for the warm bed, or a comfortable chair, and a persistent reluctance to a kneeling position.

122

If such suggestions are overcome, then the mind will put forward attractive alternatives such as looking at the latest copy of Time or reading a book. Body and mind have just as little enthusiasm for worship. The mind will make repeated, and successful, attempts to escape from church, and the body will propose that sermon time is ideal for a quiet sleep. Insomnia is unknown in church.

The Christian has to face the fact that this struggle is part of the suffering of all creation, "ourselves also, who have the first-fruits of the Spirit, even we ourselves groan within ourselves, waiting for our adoption, to wit, the redemption of our body" (Rom. 8:23). The promise is much more than the expectation of deliverance from disease, weakness, and deformity; it is the prospect of having body, mind, and spirit harmonized in a common desire to do the will of God. Man's spiritual fall darkened his mind and degraded his body. When the Lord redeems a repentant sinner, He immediately restores him spiritually to union with God and gives him the Holy Spirit as a pledge of His intention to redeem him finally in body. We will then no more have bodies that have to be beaten into submission, but bodies that will find their most exquisite pleasure in being used of God. The harmony of man's environment will be matched with the harmony within him.

The weariness of the present struggle does not blur the glory of the future day. Very few Christians believe that; for our conversation is witness that our concern is with our present state of health rather than with our eternal status. The Lord is infinitely sympathetic and certainly not indifferent toward our aches and pains. He knows your heart is weak, your eyesight failing or even gone; He knows the problems of the introvert and the difficulties of the extrovert; and He knows how often you must struggle to keep awake in prayer. He understood when you fell asleep last night before you reached the Amen. And because God understands, He has revealed what shall be when redemption is complete. In the meantime, the Holy Spirit ministers with groanings that exceed those of expectant nature and of our troubled hearts.

I once stood amid the high, snow-mantled peaks of Bavaria in the breathless moments before the dawn. Above us towered the dark outline of the mighty Zugspitze which we were to climb that day. No sound disturbed the stillness as the first pink glow from the rising sun instantly removed all traces of the night, and gave to the snow and ice a peculiar warmth that was not its own. We turned our faces eastward to watch the sun begin its steady ascent from the valley until we were ourselves transformed by its morning rays, and all the weariness of our aching limbs forgotten. A new day had dawned, splendid with hope and filled with unspoiled glory.

So shall it be when Jesus reigns. Patient waiting for Him will never be in vain, and every memory of the painful struggle will forever disappear, like shadows before the rising sun, when at last we see our Saviour reigning over the creation He has redeemed.

# Chapter Seven

*Behold, my servant shall deal wisely, he shall be exalted and lifted up, and shall be very high. Like as many were astonished at thee (his visage was so marred more than any man, and his form more than the sons of men), so shall he sprinkle many nations; kings shall shut their mouths at him: for that which had not been told them shall they see; and that which they had not heard shall they understand.*

*Who hath believed our message? and to whom hath the arm of Jehovah been revealed? For he grew up before him as a tender plant, and as a root out of a dry ground: he hath no form nor comeliness; and when we see him, there is no beauty that we should desire him. He was despised and rejected of men; a man of sorrows, and acquainted with grief: and as one from whom men hide their face he was despised; and we esteemed him not.*

*Surely he hath borne our griefs, and carried our sorrows; yet we did esteem him stricken, smitten of God, and afflicted. But he was wounded for our transgressions, he was bruised for our iniquities: the chastisement of our peace was upon him; and with his stripes we are healed. All we like sheep have gone astray; we have turned everyone to his own way; and Jehovah hath laid on him the iniquity of us all....*

*Yet it pleased Jehovah to bruise him; he hath put him to grief: when thou shalt make his soul an offering for sin, he shall see his seed, he shall prolong his days, and the pleasure of Jehovah shall prosper in his hand. —Isaiah 52:13—53:6; 10*

*If any man cometh unto me, and hateth not his own father, and mother, and wife, and children, and brethren, and sisters, yes, and his own life also cannot be my disciple.*

*Whosoever doth not bear his own cross, and come after me, cannot be my disciple....*

*So therefore whosoever he be of you that renounceth not all that he hath, he cannot be my disciple. —Luke 14:26, 27, 33*

# CHRIST YOUR LORD

MEN ARE NOT USUALLY SLOW in claiming even a nodding acquaintance with the great. Nothing more than being within camera range of a famous man is enough to create an air of distinction for the photographer, and to have shaken hands with the great man himself is to stake a claim to some degree of familiarity with him even though his recollection of the incident may only be a blur of shapeless faces and a forest of hands, one of which, belonging to no one in particular, grasped his.

Christians are not so ready to talk of their acquaintance with the Lord of all things. There are two reasons for this. The first is that we are not enough concerned with Him; the second is that we are too concerned with ourselves.

If a man feels justified in a certain amount of boasting because he once stood within ten feet of the president of the United States, or traveled on the same ship as a Hollywood starlet that he never actually saw, then is it not reasonable to assume that a man has failed altogether to realize the greatness of his Saviour if he speaks very little of Him? After all, Jesus is no mean Person. In virtue of the sacrifice of Himself upon the cross, He is our Lord. Because of His holy nature, He dazzles the angelic hosts with His glory. By His magnificent victory over the Devil, He is Lord over all the dark and evil hordes of Hell. By His triumph at the cross, He is the conquering Lord who leads His followers from one miraculous victory to another. By His personal greatness, He towers over the nations until they have no more significance than an ax in the woodman's hand. Because of His infinite power, He has undertaken the reclamation of all creation and promised to restore it to its pristine glory.

It is therefore a very high privilege to be able to call Him our Lord. We might easily expect that a Christian, in any society and at any time, would eagerly look for the smallest opportunity to interrupt the conversation with the remark that he knows Jesus Christ personally. It would not be astonishing if men were to clamor for the privilege of having the slightest contact with Him, or to strain their utmost to lay legitimate claim to being a son of God. When we see Him as He is we shall of course enthusiastically acclaim Him as our Lord. But now? The most common reason why so many Christians are slow to confess Christ is that they are more concerned for themselves than they are to make Him known.

This leads to the basic question of what a Christian ought to expect when Christ is indeed his Lord. Looking into the eternal future, we can confidently count upon the final overthrow of Satan, and the whole world hushed to see our Saviour crowned. In the immediate future, we can with equal confidence expect Him to lead us daily along the triumphant trail He trod. But beside all that, what kind of experience should be expected in this world? As followers of the Lord Jesus Christ do we have a right to hope for respect and honor as servants of the King? Assuming that the Lord does daily lead us in the train of His triumph, do we also take it for granted that life will be a series of exhilarating experiences and packed with thrills? If the truth be told, many believers have a subconscious idea that a Christian fills the role of a kind of comic strip space hero or ace jet pilot who, constantly facing innumerable odds, always comes out unscathed and with a great deal of honor for himself. This gallant hero, Chris-

127

tian or fictional, has frequent brushes with death but rarely receives more than a minor flesh wound which serves to focus the limelight even more brilliantly upon him.

The pattern of what we should expect is not found in comic strips or daydreams, but in the life of our Lord Jesus Himself. All the consequences of calling Him Lord, and acting in full accord with that confession, are bluntly set before us in these two chapters of Isaiah. If Christ is our Lord, then we are His servants. Whatever other relationships may exist between us, this cannot be denied. The cost, therefore, of calling Him Lord is the admission that we are His servants and committed to do His will at any cost. The latter part of Isaiah 52 graphically describes what is involved by such an admission. The servant in this case is Christ who was the perfect Servant, absolutely submissive to His Father's will.

In verse 13 He is announced: "Behold, my servant shall deal wisely, he shall be exalted and lifted up, and shall be very high." This is as expected. The servant of the Most High is clearminded and intelligent; for he has been let into the divine mysteries. He knows the secrets of God, and deals in matters of eternal importance. He knows the way of life, and can point others to eternal bliss. He does not grope in the dark as heathen philosophers do, but has the answer to problems which baffle the moralist or perplex the psychologist. He has found the *summum bonum*, and has the ultimate solution to every enigma. Here is the ideal of the servant of the Lord that coincides with our own imaginations. It is an ideal to which a missionary may easily gravitate when he arrives in a foreign field to find the honorary title of teacher awaiting him, no matter what his qualifications really are. Wisdom and honor seem

128

to be prerequisites to which a servant of the Lord might justly lay claim. Honor is, indeed, promised, for "he shall be exalted and lifted up, and shall be very high." The verse applies particularly to Christ, but it contain the general truth that God's servant ought to deal wisely and can expect to be honored.

The verbs of verse 13 are all in the future tense, and the verbs of verse 14 are in the past tense. What is promised in verse 13 was preceded by what is described in verse 14. "His visage was so marred more than any man, and his form more than the sons of men." In another terrible sense Christ was lifted up; and when Isaiah turned to behold the Servant he was astonished, not at His glory, but at His suffering. The glory shall be: but first the cross must be.

Although most of the world's greatest artists have used imagination and ability to paint likenesses of Christ, the Scriptures reveal very little of His appearance as a man. Luke, in describing the face of Christ at the time of the transfiguration, uses the careful language of a medical doctor. "And as he was praying, the fashion of his countenance was altered." Matthew says that "his face did shine as the sun." From Luke's precise wording, we deduce that the change in our Lord's face was not merely physical but spiritual in origin. His face had the same recognizable features that the disciples knew and loved so well, but an extraordinary radiance so shone out that Matthew was reminded of the dazzling sun. And that glory on His face disclosed all the holiness of His heart.

Now and then we see a little of that glory on a human face. On the first Christmas Day I spent in China I witnessed a baptism in a city church of the mountainous west. Five or six men and women had come in from the country to witness to their new-found faith in

129

Christ. They were all farming people, whose hands were hardened by the plow and hoe, and whose faces were dried and burned by wind and sun. One by one they stood beside the water where the pastor waited to baptize them. The announcement of each name was followed by a splash of water as they descended to stand beside the pastor and confidently affirm their faith. And as they came out, their weather-beaten faces were radiant with a heavenly light that made all other features unremarkable. Maybe the Lord Himself was witness there that day, and perhaps it was the glory of His face that transformed theirs.

The other description of Christ's face is here in Isaiah. It is in striking contrast to Luke's portrayal; for as the prophet turns to behold the Servant, he is shocked by the appearance of His face which he describes in words that literally translated are: "His look, however, was in that degree disfigured to the inhuman, and His form not like a son of man's."

Once again the cause of the change is spiritual and not physical. In the awful hours that Jesus spent in the merciless hands of the Roman soldiery, His face was no doubt made almost unrecognizable by brutal hands that tore out His beard and lacerated His brow with thorns. But there is no reason to suppose that the garrison was more cruel to Christ than to any other of their unfortunate victims. They did not invent their tortures solely for Him; cruelty was a normal part of their hard lives. Terrible as the experience must have been for our Lord Jesus, the cause of His face becoming almost inhuman lies much deeper.

A man's face inevitably reveals something of his character. Abraham Lincoln is said to have refused to receive a visitor because he did not like his face, and when it was suggested that the unfortunate caller could not help his face, the president retorted, "After forty every man is responsible for his face!" In a measure, that is true. Upon our faces courage and intelligence write their noble lines, pride and deceitfulness tell their story, and fear and worry etch their indelible marks. Determination or honesty, lust or cruelty, weakness or strength cannot be altogether hidden in the heart for they advertise themselves upon our faces. We have only to compare the sweet, innocent face of a baby with the crinkled countenance of an old man to realize that much happens between birth and death. Our faces tell the story.

An artist who had been commissioned to paint The Last Supper, having lightly sketched in the background of his picture, began work upon his conception of the twelve apostles, seated around the table. For a likeness of John, the artist decided to look for a man whose holy and refined face would suggest to him the disciple who leaned upon the bosom of Christ. Out into the streets of the city he went until he found a man who filled the part, and using him as a model, he painted in the face of John. The completion of the work was delayed for several years, but once more the painter took up his brushes and painted steadily until only one of the Twelve remained. The twelfth was Judas Iscariot, whom the artist had purposely left until last, knowing that his face must be altogether different from those of the other disciples. Imagination failed him, and once more he decided to go out into the streets of the city in search of a man that appeared to be abandoned to evil. In a filthy alley be came upon a man whose furtive manner and hard, deceitful face suggested a likeness of Judas, and without difficulty persuaded him to sit for his portrait in return for liberal payment. Together they went to where the unfinished picture stood, and seating his dissolute model nearby, the artist began to paint in the features of the betrayer. But he had made only a few swift strokes with his brush, when the man pointed to the face of John, and cried out with a despairing sob, "O God, that's me!" Life in a wicked city had changed him from a John to a Judas, and the story was written on his face.

Behold the face of Jesus in His agony, and you will see the story of mankind. Our transgressions and our iniquities marred His face when His soul was made an offering for sin. His own immaculate holiness was the cause of His face being transfigured on the mountain; our incorrigible sin was the cause of His face being disfigured on the cross.

The awful change in the face of Christ may have taken place in the Garden of Gethsemane when three times over He prayed, "Not my will, but thine be done." The words seem to make a sharp distinction between the will of Christ and the will of His Father. Accepting one involved a repudiation of the other, and since He and His Father were at all times in complete harmony and unanimity of purpose, it is all the more remarkable that at the great crisis of His human life, the Lord should speak as if His will was different from that of His Father. To understand that difference is to understand the measure and meaning of His suffering. The will of Christ was righteousness. Of Him alone it is written that He "loved righteousness and hated iniquity," and in consequence He was the happiest Man who ever lived; for "God, thy God, hath anointed thee with the oil of gladness above thy fellows" (Heb. 1:9). It is as difficult to appreciate what it means to love righteousness and hate iniquity as to imagine what it would be like to live on the moon where the pull of gravity is only one-sixth that of earth. Men by nature hate righteousness and love iniquity, and even the saints have been horrified to find with Moses that sin is pleasurable. Many of our problems and struggles as Christians can be traced back to the fact that we love righteousness too little and sin too much. Jesus was different. Sin constantly repelled Him, and righteousness unfailingly attracted Him. As a little child, all through His boyhood and even in the difficult teenage years, He loved to do what was right in the sight of God. Righteousness for Him was not merely an obligation, it was His pleasure. As a man, He consistently hated sin with a deep loathing and pursued righteousness with unchanging desire. That was His will.

God's will for His Son's earthly life was certainly righteousness but His will for His Son's death was altogether different. He planned to lay on Christ the iniquity of us all, and make Him to be sin on our behalf. Jesus was to be made what He most abhorred. Loving righteousness, He was to be made sin. His personal will as perfect Man was to surrender to the Father's will which was that He should accept to the full the guilt of imperfect men. And just as the perfection of holiness transfigured His face with radiant glory on the mount, so the very essence of evil that He became for us transformed His face on another mount until it was unlike the face of any man that ever lived. No more terrible words in all literature can be found than the stark declaration of Scripture that "he hath made him to be sin." "Behold, my servant," says the Lord, and seeing Him you will begin to understand that the way to glory is via a cross.

Outside one of the mountain cities of western China, there was a colony of about seventy lepers. During the war, China was cut off from the rest of the world by Japanese encirclement, and very little help

133

could be given to the unfortunate men and women who suffered there. A local church generously contributed to the building of a small chapel in the colony, and through the faithful ministry of the pastor and church members most of the lepers accepted Christ as Savior.

The pastor and I were close friends, and I often enjoyed going out to assist him in his ministry to that pathetic flock. Imaginative descriptions of the leper by preachers at home are inadequate preparation for sitting in a small chapel on a hot summer's day with a crowd of men and women whose rotting bodies filled the place with the stench of death. Fingerless hands were stretched out in imploring prayer that was spoken through great swollen lips. Some sat as they prayed: they had no feet to stand on. Many had large festering sores, partially covered with brown paper through which blood and pus oozed. China was desperately short of medical supplies in those days, and all that could be flown in were urgently needed for the fighting men who fell in battle. One Wednesday when the Chinese pastor and I arrived, the usual crowd had gathered at the entrance to welcome us. As we stood talking in the sunshine, a woman came across the fields leading a girl of about twelve years old. Pointing to a small sore on the girl's left foot, the mother explained that it had been diagnosed as leprosy, and that she had been told to bring her daughter to the colony. There was a long, long silence as the lepers looked at the pretty little girl, and the girl looked in horror at the bodies and the faces of the lepers. Then, in one awful moment of desperate understanding, the terrible truth broke upon her that she would inevitably become like them.

For Jesus it was more than that. He did not only become like us; He became sin. It was as if all the sin in all the world, and from every generation, was suddenly concentrated in one Person who willingly made Himself responsible for the whole. And the exceeding greatness of the awful burden so distorted His face with agony that He was made unrecognizable.

If this happened to our Lord, what then should His servants expect? Most of our modern Christian ditties emphasize sentimental, happy themes and avoid the reality of suffering. The hymn that old Isaac Watts wrote to challenge happy-go-lucky believers of his day would not go over so well in our generation.

> Am I a soldier of the cross,
> A follower of the Lamb,
> And shall I fear to own His cause,
> Or blush to speak His name?
> Must I be carried to the skies,
> On flowry beds of ease,
> While others fought to win the prize,
> And sailed through bloody seas?

Although we are thrilled with a Lord who is the mighty conqueror of Satan, and who deals with nations as a man might swat an irritating little bug, we have little enthusiasm for following Him along the bloody trail He trod. But in all Scripture there is no suggestion whatever that a believer should expect better treatment in this world than his Lord. Since He was despised, then you should be despised too, for He is your Lord. He was rejected of men; then why not you? His coronation in glory was preceded by the shame of the cross, and if He is to be your Lord, then this is the way you must go. We do not, and cannot, have any share in His suffering for the sins of the world, but the source of our suffering is the same as His. It comes from a world that is resolutely determined that Christ shall never be Lord. And while we assert with all our strength that Christ died for our sins, and not merely to show men how to die or to give a supreme example of self-sacrifice for a great cause, yet dogmatically proclaiming that great truth must never blind us to the other truth that "Christ also suffered for you, leaving you an example, that ye should follow his steps" (I Peter 2:21).

To come to Christ costs nothing; and yet it costs everything. Any man can be saved from the guilt and power of sin at no cost except the price of humbling himself by a confession that he is a helpless sinner in God's sight, and accepting Christ as his Saviour. But in doing that, Christ becomes his Lord. The man loses his sins, but he also loses his rights. He has done more than accept Christ: He has received the Lord Jesus Christ "who is the blessed and only Potentate, the King of kings, and Lord of lords."

The attractive idea has always been popular that a man can be saved on his own terms. Examples could be given of churches that have built up large congregations by the simple device of cutting out any conditions for salvation that might offend prospective church members, especially the wealthy class. God's minima for salvation cannot be reduced to meet man's convenience. Romans 10:9 is a favorite memory verse, but not so well used as conditions for church membership. "If thou shalt confess with thy mouth Jesus as Lord, and shalt believe in thy heart that God raised him from the dead, thou shalt be saved." Much is included or implied in those few words. Salvation is the consequence of faith that is deep in the heart and not merely an intellectual assent to the Gospel. Such a faith unconditionally accepts the resurrection of Jesus Christ, and God's power to work miracles. And such a faith includes an open confession that Christ is Lord. From this verse it could even be argued that willingness to accept Christ as Lord

136

is an essential condition of having Him as Saviour. There is certainly no suggestion that at conversion Christ becomes our Saviour, but that we retain the option of making Him our Lord at our convenience. We have no choice. Since He is Lord and Saviour, accepting Him as the one necessitates His becoming the other. A child might as well decide to accept one of its parents as father, but defer until later a decision regarding its mother. When we accepted Christ, He became our Lord. Recognition of that fact is a point of controversy that often centers on a particular item over which you and God disagree, but the real issue is not whether you should or should not do something or other, but whether Christ is your Lord indeed.

No spiritual progress takes place until this point is settled. If God is to commission you for His royal service, as He commissioned Isaiah, then He first must be your Lord. If you have ever wondered why the Lord does not use you, the probable answer is that you do not regard Him as your Lord. If He is to lead you to victory, as He led Israel in Isaiah's days, then He first must be your Lord. If you are to enjoy peace in knowing that Christ rules over the nations and will redeem all creation, then first He must be your Lord. All weak Christianity can be traced back to the fact that Christ is not recognized as Lord. The complaint was once made by a church member that things are coming to a fine pass when religion begins to interfere with personal affairs, and the reason why so few Christians experience victory and power is that they prefer to manage their own lives, and suit their religion to their own convenience.

No one need be in any doubt as to whether Christ is his Lord or not. The Scriptures supply a triple test. "If any man cometh unto me, and hateth not his own

137

father, and mother, and wife, and children, and brethren, and sisters, yea, and his own life also, he cannot be my disciple. Whosoever doth not bear his own cross, and come after me, cannot be my disciple.... Whosoever he be of you that renounceth not all that he hath, he cannot be my disciple" (Luke 14:26, 27, 33). The first of those three verses makes it perfectly clear that coming to Christ involves an exacting condition. The invitation at evangelistic services to come to Christ is sometimes given as if acceptance is to do God a favor, or conversely, as if a response to the invitation is a means by which we obtain untold blessings and God obtains nothing. The solemn truth is that it is possible to come to Christ and be rejected. "If any man cometh unto me, and hateth not his own father . . . he cannot be my disciple." We come to Christ on His terms, or not at all.

The acid test of the cross is applied first to the family relationship. The language is strong and appears harsh. If a man would be a disciple of Christ, then he must hate the dearest members of his own family. What we hate, we reject; what we love, we choose. For example, I might say that I love to fly but I hate to travel by ship, which means that when I have the choice—and the money!—I always choose the plane in preference to the ship. And if Christ is my Lord, then I will always choose His will even if that conflicts with what my parents, family, wife, or children want. Such a choice may easily give the impression that I have not love for my own family. Very few Chinese or Japanese who accept Christ as Saviour and Lord can escape the suffering of this choice. As soon as the new believer refuses to join in family worship before the Buddhist altar, where prayers and food and incense are offered to the spirits of the departed, he will be accused of not caring for his family. The word will get around that he has no love for his ancestors, and his parents will accuse him of being without affection for them since he has repudiated his filial duty of ministering to their spirits after death. To a non-Christian community, no clearer evidence of hatred of the family could exist: for the most sacred duty of a son is being refused.

The choice can be just as difficult for young people in our own country. God's call to a young man to serve Him in the obscurity of a foreign mission field may involve the loss of a promising career that his father has lovingly prepared for him. A girl may have to make a choice between a comfortable marriage with the prospect of an easy life at home, and the long loneliness of life in a land where Christ is not known and husbands are not easily found. Some might judge that an only son, who forsakes his parents to go out and expose himself to all the dangers of a disease-ridden tropical country whose fanatical people are openly hostile to missionaries, is lacking in love for his parents. The standard of judgment is a cross. Christ Himself, the only begotten Son, chose to leave His Father, face the virulent hatred of a world in revolt against Him, and die amid a scoffing mob. And if He is indeed our Lord, then He will be given priority over all our family interests.

The second test goes deeper. "His own life also," and "whosoever doth not bear his own cross, and come after me, cannot be my disciple." Hating our own lives and bearing our cross is equivalent to coming after Christ. He comes first, and I come after.

The strongest of all instincts is self-preservation. Only saints and heroes scorn danger. The majority of men instinctively exert all their strength to save themselves from death, and recoil quickly from any threat to their precious selves. We react sharply to criticism,

139

mockery, ostracism, loss of face, or anything else that might whittle away our social standing or prestige. We dread the thought of being considered unscientific, and preachers concerned with the preservation of their reputation as men of the twentieth century blanch at the danger of being called medieval obscurantists. At all costs, we struggle to guard our reputation. But ask what your Lord did when faced with a similar choice, and the answer will come back clear and strong that He "made himself of no reputation," but was willing to be "despised and rejected of men."

Since making Christ Lord cuts at the very root of our strongest instinct, we try to hold out against Him. We fear what will happen to us if we accept Him unconditionally as Lord. It will be the end of us. That is why our Lord plainly said that to follow Him involves bearing our cross. It is our cross in the sense that we make the decision that, even though the cost be our lives, Christ shall come first. Pain that touches the very core of our being, which could be avoided by the easy choice of caring most for ourselves, is the hardest to bear. But discipleship is on no other terms.

Men offering for military service are not accepted conditionally. Suppose, for example, that a man should insist that he must not be sent overseas, or more than fifty miles from home; that he must not be given any unpleasant duty or asked to fight; that he be required to report for duty only from 1100 to 1200 hours on Sundays and from 2000 to 2100 hours on Wednesday, and that he only wear his uniform on those two occasions; and that, finally, he be given the Congressional Medal of Honor after eighteen months and discharged with full pay so that be might devote the rest of his life to recounting tales of his heroism, or perhaps to writing a book. The volunteer, if such he could be called, would probably be referred to a soap opera company, if the sergeant could control himself sufficiently to suggest anything so polite.

Christians, in fact, demand such conditions of Him they dare to address as Lord. The Sunday service (morning but not evening), and occasionally the Wednesday evening prayer meeting (where they can be counted on to give a good prayer beginning, "O Lord") are the most they are willing to offer, and they feel they have every right to insist they must not be sent overseas or expected to witness for Christ anywhere except within the friendly security of the church. They are expecting full honors on retirement, and perhaps secretly look forward to the day when they can recount their terrific adventures as soldiers of the cross.

During the last war, a popular magazine carried a picture of a group of Russian antitank gunners, standing in a circle and holding their weapons high above their heads, as they solemnly held a ceremony to bid farewell to life. And the blunt truth is that unless we are prepared to follow Christ, even at the cost of our lives, we not only are not His disciples, but cannot be.

As the dark shadows of Communism remorselessly creep over the face of the earth, more and more Christians have to choose between their own lives and Christ. During a time of intense pressure and danger, a Chinese Christian leader wrote to his fellow pastors a letter that included the following paragraph:

If we are unwilling to disregard our life or our death, we cannot be faithful to God, and cannot serve Him. If we do not have this will, and we are threatened by men, we are apt to immediately fall. How shall such a shepherd feed the flock? How shall he be a valiant keeper of the Truth, a valiant Christian soldier? If you are willing to be a good shepherd of the flock and

141

a good soldier under the banner of Christ, you must, like Paul, die daily. If the Lord does not allow you to die, you, in the evening, kneel down to thank Him for His preservation and protection. Having slept a night, you awaken the following morning to again prepare to die. Look at the great number of preachers who today covet life and are afraid to die. They have lost their loyalty to God, and before men they have lost their witness. They have, in fear and nervousness, joined the world. Though they still live, it would have been better for them had they died already. With such a life of shamefulness bringing sorrow to God, what can the benefits of life be?

Those are the words of a man to whom Christ is Lord indeed.

The third test touches our possessions. "Whosoever he be of you that renounceth not all that he hath, he cannot be my disciple." The Lord does not ask that we give away all that we have, but that we abandon any right to what we have. Christ, and not our possessions, masters us.

I retain a vivid recollection of setting out to China as a young missionary in the war year of 1939. All that I possessed in the world was securely stowed away in seven boxes somewhere in the hold of the ship. By hours of thought and careful planning, I had reduced my equipment to the basic essentials without which I honestly believed I could not efficiently operate. I did not realize how much my things meant to me until a German submarine sneaked within two hundred yards of our ship. The swift appearance of a destroyer saved us. The dark hull of the sub was blown clear out of the water by the force of the depth charge, but I began to think over what would have happened if my boxes, instead of the German raider, had sunk to the bottom of the Atlantic. Less than a year later a new threat arose when a band of robbers were rumored to be near the little town in West China where we had been sent for language study. The seven boxes became a major source of anxiety, and I discovered that the fewer our possessions, the more precious they are. The issue went deeper. Did I possess the things, or the things possess me? Who was my master, the seven boxes or Christ? The solution was obvious. Renounce all that I had and be Christ's unencumbered disciple. Peace came when all that I had was handed back to Christ the Lord for Him to do whatever seemed good, and about two years later there was no pain at the almost total loss of the seven precious boxes.

When Christ is Lord indeed, He comes before family, before possessions, and before my very life.

A natural reaction to this truth is that the cost of recognizing Him as Lord is far too high. Complacent Christianity prefers to bury its head in the warm sands of orthodox ineffectiveness. We choose rather to squander our wealth on luxuries and, to be quite honest, we find it less disturbing to listen to the radio than to Christ, and less demanding to watch TV than look into the Scriptures. The Lord Jesus Himself openly warned men that they must face all that is involved in being His disciples before starting out. "Which of you desiring to build a tower, doth not first sit down and count the cost," and "what king, as he goeth to encounter another king in war, will not sit down first and take counsel whether he is able with ten thousand to meet him that cometh against him with twenty thousand?" (Luke 14: 28, 31). We might see a better caliber of Christian today if there were less standing up in the excitement of an emotional church service, and more sitting down to consider carefully whether Christ is to have

143

everything or not. Even God cannot build a strong Christian character when He is denied access to most of the materials, and the reason for so many believers never reaching maturity, but fading out completely, is that Christ was never made Lord of all.

The reason for defeat is often the same. Since believers are usually outnumbered, victory depends on skillful leadership. We are seldom in as favorable a position as having ten thousand to put against the enemy's twenty thousand. The odds against us are more often about ten to one, and if we are to conquer, Christ must be in full command of all our faculties, gifts, bodies, and possessions. When He is given all, He leads to certain victory; when He is given less than everything, He makes no guarantee of deliverance. The price of independence is defeat.

But the cost of yielding all to Christ must ultimately be considered in the light of the price He paid to redeem us. Neither in eternity nor in time, neither in Heaven nor on earth did Christ falter in His determination to renounce all that He had, hate His own life also, and take up His cross and go steadfastly to Calvary.

When England stood tensely expecting the full fury of a German onslaught in the early days of World War II, Winston Churchill, in a speech of heroic defiance, had nothing to offer his beloved land but blood, and sweat, and tears until the day of victory should dawn at last. Jesus offers us no less, but promises us much more. The Servant whose face was so marred that it was beyond human semblance was to be "exalted and lifted up, and shall be very high." And so shall we, if we walk His way.

In the old days of the Scottish Covenanters, it was the custom of some believers to enter into an agreement with God which they deliberately set down on paper. One of these old covenants has been preserved for us, and its careful wording records the full surrender of a heart and life to Christ the Lord. It reads:

> *I hereby give my hearty consent, Lord Jesus, to Thy coming in and taking possession of my soul, and to Thy casting out of everything there that stands in opposition to Thee. I desire Thee for my all, to be ruled and governed by Thee, acquiescing to whatsoever shall be Thy way of dealing with me. Give me Thyself, and Thou shalt be all my desire.*

In the final days of the war, Japan called for men to pilot suicide planes which were no more than winged bombs flown right into the target. The men who flew the little planes on a one-way mission to certain death were called the Kamikaze or Divine Wind pilots. Their single passion was to die for the glory of their Emperor and the honor of their country. In the dying days of this old world, the hosts of darkness are massed for their final, desperate stand against the Lord of hosts. The outcome is certain. Satan shall be defeated; the nations shall be subjugated, and Christ shall reign. But until that great and glorious day shall dawn, God is looking for kamikaze men who with daring faith will abandon all for Him, caring nothing save only this, Jesus shall be Lord.